estherpress

Books for Courageous Women

ESTHER PRESS VISION

Publishing diverse voices that encourage and equip women to walk courageously in the light of God's truth for such a time as this.

BIBLICAL STATEMENT OF PURPOSE

"For if you keep silent at this time, relief and deliverance will rise for the Jews from another place, but you and your father's house will perish. And who knows whether you have not come to the kingdom for such a time as this?"

Esther 4:14 (ESV)

What people are saying about …

THE PROMISED PRESENCE

"Jenny Randle does what few women, in my opinion, are able to do with the Word of God and teaches us the simplicity and power if we will just open our Bibles and let God speak. *The Promised Presence* is an invitation to explore a topic personally and corporately that is often avoided, leading us on a journey to understanding the presence of God is a gift for every believer, regardless of our faith journey."

Natalie Runion, bestselling author and founder of Raised to Stay

"There are those who know much about the Holy Spirit, and there are those who know Him personally. Jenny Randle is both. A student of the Word and the Spirit, Jenny is well-equipped to share this important message and offer this powerful resource for the body of Christ. *The Promised Presence* is an invitation for those who are desperate to see God move in power and long to encounter the Holy Spirit in a way that enables them to walk fully in what Jesus' sacrifice made available to them. I believe this book is an invitation absolutely worth accepting, and I'm so grateful for Jenny's voice in this hour."

Becky Thompson, author of *God So Close*

"I love how Jenny Randle not only *invites* us into a deeper understanding of the Holy Spirit but also *leads* us into His presence. She takes us by the hand and gives us an up-front, personal introduction to the Holy Spirit. In the process, Jenny helps us to know Him as the powerful

Comforter and gentle Teacher He was meant to be for us. After reading this book, you will walk away with a renewed sense of wonder and awe of God."

Amy Elaine Martinez, author, speaker, podcast host of *The Grace Frontier*, former radio show host

"In *The Promised Presence*, Jenny Randle invites us on a life-changing journey through Luke and Acts, helping us experience the Holy Spirit's power and authority in a fresh, deeply personal way. With biblical wisdom and engaging storytelling, she leads us to embrace the presence of God, not as a distant concept, but as an ever-present companion who empowers, guides, and transforms our lives. If you long to walk in greater faith, boldness, and intimacy with the Holy Spirit, this book is a must-read. Jenny's words will inspire you to step into the fullness of God's promises with confidence and joy!"

Dr. Michelle Bengtson, clinical neuropsychologist, speaker, author of *Breaking Anxiety's Grip* and *The Hem of His Garment*, and host of *Your Hope-Filled Perspective* podcast

"I believe that God welcomes our questions and even our doubts. I have had many questions about the Holy Spirit since I was a child at the altar of my Pentecostal church. I wanted everything the Holy Spirit had for me, but I honestly wasn't sure what that meant. I wish I had Jenny Randle's book *The Promised Presence* decades ago. As I read through her manuscript, I laughed and I cried—and I also felt safe. If you have wondered who the Holy Spirit is and what exactly the presence of the Holy Spirit brings to one's life, wonder no longer. You will breathe a sigh of relief and contentment as you travel through the pages of Scripture with Jenny."

Carol McLeod, Bible teacher, podcaster, and author

"Jenny brings biblical wisdom, infectious enthusiasm, and powerful personal testimonies as she invites us into a deeper relationship with Holy Spirit. This study provides a framework with sound scriptural insight that helps awaken our souls to the Spirit's active and pervasive influence in every aspect of our lives. Whether you're a sage in the faith or just beginning your journey, this book will invigorate your life and fan the flames of your faith."

Kellie Haddock, singer-songwriter

"Every believer needs to know the transformational power of the miracle-working Holy Spirit. Yet, so many Christians are underdeveloped in their understanding. In this beautiful book, Jenny delivers a powerful and comprehensive study of His work. You will be drawn in right away by Jenny's personal stories. This is a must-read for everyone who desires a deeper experience of God's presence."

Becky Harling, conference speaker, leadership coach, and author of fifteen books including *Cultivating Deeper Connections in a Lonely World*

"*The Promised Presence* is a thorough yet practical guide for anyone wanting to learn more about who the Holy Spirit is and how the Spirit works in the lives of believers. This book will not only help you to increase your knowledge of the Holy Spirit but will lead you toward experiencing the presence and power of the Spirit in your everyday life."

Blake Snapp, lead pastor of Christwalk Church, Fernandina Beach, Florida

"*The Promised Presence* is a practical and powerful guide, offering a much-needed resource for women who are seeking a deeper connection and understanding of their relationship with the Holy Spirit. Its practicality is made known through the well-thought-out tools, guiding questions, and creative layout, while the power is evident in the Scripture references and the raw, real testimonies of walking out the refining, powerful, hard, and sanctifying life surrendered to the Holy Spirit. I highly recommend this book as a valuable resource in every Christian woman's library."

Avery Forrest, associate pastor of Anchor Point Church

THE PROMISED PRESENCE

AN INTERACTIVE BOOK
WITH FIVE SESSIONS
OF VIDEO INCLUDED

JENNY RANDLE

THE PROMISED PRESENCE

AN INTRODUCTION TO HOLY SPIRIT'S POWER AND AUTHORITY

A JOURNEY THROUGH LUKE AND ACTS

150 YEARS STRONG
DAVID C COOK

THE PROMISED PRESENCE
Published by Esther Press,
an imprint of David C Cook
4050 Lee Vance Drive
Colorado Springs, CO 80918 U.S.A.

Integrity Music Limited, a Division of David C Cook
Brighton, East Sussex BN1 2RE, England

Esther Press®, the EP logo, DAVID C COOK® and related marks are registered trademarks of David C Cook.

All rights reserved. Except for brief excerpts for review purposes,
no part of this book may be reproduced or used in any form
without written permission from the publisher.

The website addresses recommended throughout this book are offered as a resource to you. These websites are not intended in any way to be or imply an endorsement on the part of David C Cook, nor do we vouch for their content.

The following work of nonfiction recounts events, people, dates, and medical information
to the best of the author's ability. To maintain the anonymity of others, some names in
this book have been changed to protect the privacy of the individuals.

Unless otherwise noted, all Scripture quotations are taken from the ESV® Bible (The Holy Bible, English Standard Version®), copyright © 2001 by Crossway, a publishing ministry of Good News Publishers. Used by permission. All rights reserved. Scripture quotations marked NIV are taken from the Holy Bible, New International Version®, NIV®. Copyright © 1973, 2011 by Biblica, Inc.™ Used by permission of Zondervan. All rights reserved worldwide. www.zondervan.com. The "NIV" and "New International Version" are trademarks registered in the United States Patent and Trademark Office by Biblica, Inc.™ Scripture quotations marked NLT are taken from the Holy Bible, New Living Translation, copyright © 1996, 2015 by Tyndale House Foundation. Used by permission of Tyndale House Publishers, Carol Stream, Illinois 60188. All rights reserved. The author has added italics and bold to Scripture quotations for emphasis.

ISBN 978-0-8307-8592-6
eISBN 978-0-8307-8621-3

© 2025 Jenny Randle

The Team: Susan McPherson, Marianne Herring, Stephanie Bennett, James Hershberger, Jack Campbell, Susan Murdock
Cover Design: Micah Kandros
Author Cover Bio Photo: Brookshier Creative

Printed in the United States of America
First Edition 2025

1 2 3 4 5 6 7 8 9 10

030525

To my dad and mom

One is the adventurer jumping through hoops of fire, the other offering a safe place to land. You make a great team and have set the foundation of courage, love, and endurance our family has been built upon. This book is dedicated to you—for sitting in the bleachers every game, even when I sat the bench.

"We must be women desperately inhaling the breath of God and deliberately exhaling the things that aren't of Him. As the Spirit blows, the coals of our souls begin to flicker again. We burn for Christ, with embers catching the wind ignited to fully live."

Jenny Randle

CONTENTS

Meet the Author 17
Inside These Pages 19
A Note from Jenny 23

Week 1 Pre-Session Questions and Teaching Video
Week 1: The Wonder of God's Spirit

Day 1: Mysteries of the Miraculous: How do I see God's perspective in the unseen plans? ... 41
Day 2: Miracles in Luke: Where is Holy Spirit's involvement in Jesus' earthly ministry? ... 45
Day 3: My Wonder List: How can I sustain a sense of wonder if I'm overwhelmed? ... 51
Day 4: Mighty Acts: How are ordinary believers empowered to do extraordinary things? ... 57
Day 5: Miracles in Life and Death: What does God's provision look like in pain? ... 63

Week 2 Pre-Session Questions and Teaching Video
Week 2: The Present Reality of God's Spirit

Day 1: Promises in Luke: What gift does Jesus promise to those who follow Him? ... 79
Day 2: Permanent Resident: How do I know if God's Spirit is with me? ... 83
Day 3: Clash of Kingdoms: How does God stabilize me during spiritual warfare? ... 87
Day 4: Deceptions from Connection: What holds me back from knowing Holy Spirit? ... 93
Day 5: Acts of Proclamation: Why is Holy Spirit with me? ... 99

Week 3 Pre-Session Questions and Teaching Video
Week 3: The Fellowship of God's Spirit

Day 1: Indwelled by Love: What's the heart of the matter? ... 115
Day 2: Baptized with God's Promise: Why is Pentecost important today? ... 121

Day 3: Filled with God's Presence: How do post-conversion encounters equip me? 127
Day 4: Sanctified to Be Set Apart: How does developing godly fruit make a difference? 131
Day 5: Transformed to Be Free: What does biblical deliverance look like? 135

Week 4 Pre-Session Questions and Teaching Video
Week 4: The Powerful Work of God's Spirit

Day 1: In Sickness and in Health: How does God's Spirit minister healing? 155
Day 2: In the Secret Place: How does spending time with God's Spirit in private change me? 159
Day 3: In the Sacred Church: How does Holy Spirit's ministry strengthen my church? 163
Day 4: In Surrendered Participation: Where can God use me? 167
Day 5: In the Standstill: What if I don't have my happy ending on this side of eternity? 173

Week 5 Pre-Session Questions and Teaching Video

Final Exhortation 183
Bonus Material: Common Questions 185
    For the Theologians: What is the role of the Spirit in the Old Testament believer?
    For the Mentors: How can I help others hear and respond to Holy Spirit?
    For the Advocates: How do I pray for the sick?
    For the Warriors: How can I help others find freedom?
    For the Intercessors: Should I pray for Holy Spirit to fill others?
    For the Gifted: How do I operate in my spiritual gifting?
    For the Firecrackers: What does my authority look like as a Christ follower?
Acknowledgments 199
Appendix of Figures 201
Glossary 205
Notes 213

Scan the QR code below with your phone's camera, or visit the following URL and enter the access code to unlock Jenny Randle's five-part teaching series.

URL: davidccook.org/access

Code: Presence

For additional resources, visit jennyrandle.com/presence.

Lesson 1 Teaching: The Awe in the Already and Not Yet	28
Lesson 2 Teaching: The Unseen Life	68
Lesson 3 Teaching: Holy Spirit and God's People	106
Lesson 4 Teaching: Private Spaces and Public Places	142
Lesson 5 Teaching: Walk by the Spirit	180

MEET THE AUTHOR

Jenny Randle is an Emmy®-award-winning editor who went on a journey to discover what it really means to live on purpose. From a video editor in the heart of Hollywood to becoming an ordained minister, her creative ventures have reached millions. She has cohosted a fun and top-ranked podcast, *Shut the Should Up*, authored *Courageous Creative, Getting to Know God's Voice,* and *Dream Come True (Harvest House),* and coauthored *Flash Theology (David C Cook).* She speaks around the nation, encouraging people to live out the practical ministry and proper theology of Holy Spirit with strength and stability.

Jenny holds an MA in Biblical and Theological Foundations (Asbury Theological Seminary) and a BS in Television/Radio (Ithaca College). She has been in vocational ministry for over fifteen years, working with local churches and international ministries. She is the president of the Holy Spirit Ministry Center, an organization providing prayer, resources, and training classes to help Christ followers and those searching for truth experience Holy Spirit's presence, power, and purpose.

Jenny and her husband, Matt, live on an island in northern Florida with their two middle-school-aged kids, Max and Zoey. Jenny is all about celebrating Christ's redemptive work in our lives. To invite her to speak, view Jenny's statement of faith, or to join the party, grab the confetti and find encouragement at **jennyrandle.com**.

INSIDE THESE PAGES

The Promised Presence can be used for individual reading, personal Bible study, or as a small group experience. In the book, I share personal devotion, reflection, and Bible study surrounding the work of God's Spirit.

This book contains four sessions (also called "weeks") with five lessons in each week. Every week starts with **Pre-Session Questions and Teaching Video** for church small groups, book clubs, or deeper individual reflection. If your group wants more discussion questions, you can also review the daily questions together. The **Pre-Session Questions and Teaching Video** follows a five-week format that pushes the conversation forward. There's also additional material at the end of the book. This includes the final group session and **Common Questions**.

You may notice when I write about Holy Spirit, I often drop the "the." This is intentional as it personalizes the person of God—Father God, Lord Jesus, Holy Spirit. Although my theology-loving brain can understand why the Greek language uses definite articles such as "the," regardless of where you stand in this low-key debate, know my prayers aren't focused on that but on two things. During our time together, let's pray this resource assists women in developing their relationship with a personal God and that Holy Spirit's power and authority are evident and actively moving through you, your family, and your local church.

Are you ready to sit with the Scripture, prayerfully contemplate questions throughout each lesson, and lean in and listen to a God who loves you deeply?

Scan the QR code below with your phone's camera, or visit the following URL and enter the access code to unlock Jenny Randle's five-part teaching series.

URL: davidccook.org/access

Code: Presence

For additional resources, visit jennyrandle.com/presence.

Our Scripture will study Luke and Acts. Some scholars believe the author wrote Luke–Acts as one continuous book. We won't be going through the biblical text exegetically (line by line). Instead, our focus is a topical approach regarding Holy Spirit's power and authority in connection to Jesus' earthly ministry and the expansion of the early church. In the gospel of Luke, the story progresses to Jerusalem, the center of Judaism, from around 6 BC–AD 30.[1] In Acts, it progresses toward Rome, center of the Roman Empire and the known world, from AD 30–AD 62.[2]

For all those visual learners out there, I've incorporated plenty of charts throughout this book. Skipping the charts is like trying to assemble furniture without the instructions. Don't risk a wobbly foundation! Read the charts to properly build your theology of God's Spirit.

Figure 1. Understanding of Luke-Acts

Comparison of Luke's writings in the Bible

GOSPEL OF LUKE	ACTS
Written by Luke to Theophilus, which means "friend" or "beloved of God"[3] Luke was a Gentile, physician (Col. 4:14), historian, and companion and coworker of Paul (Philem. 24)	
Written: In the early AD 60s, after Mark[4]	**Written:** Sometime in AD 62–64[5]
Type of book: Biography of Jesus	**Type of book:** Historical narrative
Focus: Humanity of Jesus	**Focus:** Holy Spirit
Main Ideas: To show the broad Gentile audience the historical accounts of the life of Jesus are literal and trustworthy

To share that Gentile Christians can be conformed into image bearers of God | **Main Ideas:** To show the Greeks how the Way, Christianity, includes them

To share eyewitness accounts of the early church filled with the supernatural power of God as they spread the gospel |

A NOTE FROM JENNY

Dear Reader,

This book is for those who know there's more to life than what we see in front of us. *The Promised Presence* is a real and raw plea to a God who brings life to dead things. I share this because it's my story.

    Years ago, there was a season of deep loneliness in my life. It wasn't that I lacked community or connection; it was because I didn't want to bare my soul to them. My soul felt too tender to share the failure I thought I was facing. It was as if keeping my own pain was keeping me safe, but I ended up isolating myself in the process. I decided to reach out to a few of my close friends I felt safe with. I shared my dirt with them, and we sat in the mud as we tried to make sense of it all. Together, we searched for glimpses of God's goodness. Around the same time, I felt God remind me not to forsake the gathering of the saints. So, I went and wept at my local church and received pastoral counsel. The process was tender and like tilling the soil as if we were getting the ground ready to plant something that would eventually bloom.

    I remember texting an SOS to one of my besties, Britt. I knew I was sending my text when she was getting dinner on the table for the kids, but she answered anyway. Between my ugly cries, Britt listened as I replayed a hard situation I was up against. I ended with, "Please tell me I have to keep going."

    "You will keep going. You can't give up!" she said firmly.

    You can't give up either.

I know life is heavy. The heaviness weighing me down in my own health mystery and private pain boils down to a question perhaps you've wondered too. **Where is God? Can I trust Him with this one precious life He's given me?**

As I do with all my projects, I process through them with my husband, Matt. He knows I've been actively learning about God's Spirit since before our days of leading ministry for college students in 2007. In hearing what I set out to write and the big question I was tackling, Matt asked, "What if you don't get the happy ending you're hoping for?" I did what every logical, busy mama-bear-full-time-seminarian who's also working would do—I compartmentalized his question, shoving it into a corner for later. I've since found the "what-ifs" are like torturous scratches moving down the old-school chalkboard.

> *The Promised Presence* is a real and raw plea to a God who brings life to dead things.

My theology tells me God isn't a stagnant or careless God. He's a God of precision, like a surgeon. He sees an opportunity to cut as an opportunity to heal. He needs me to lie still, exposing my wounds so He can bring repair. He's a God who doesn't wish ill upon me or want to doom and gloom me to the grave. He's a just, grace-filled, and compassionate God. He's a God who loves and leads to repentance. I know all that. I'm a woman of deep faith, but here I sit with a broken reality. I'm not crying out for practical help; I'm crying out to see the purpose-filled Helper.

I know we aren't promised a life with butterflies and rainbows every step ... but we are promised one that's secure in Christ and empowered by His Spirit. So, throughout these pages, my goal is to teach us about the power and authority of Holy Spirit through biblical truth while sharing my own real story. May it encourage you to feel safe enough to share your real story too.

You aren't alone, and God turns messes into miracles all the time. Let's go search for the miracles together. I'm your SOS, urging you to unpack hard questions and keep battling to see the beautiful. I pray we find answers, stand on a firm foundation, and encounter hope together.

Love,
Jenny

WEEK 1 PRE-SESSION QUESTIONS AND TEACHING VIDEO

Community Connection

Let's briefly get to know one another. Share a little about yourself, your stage of life, and why you decided to join this group studying about Holy Spirit.

Learning Theology

- Go to page 34 and read the definition of *Holy Spirit*. Have you ever considered God's Spirit an active presence in your present reality? How does this perspective impact your daily living?
- *Pneuma* in Greek means "breathe" or "spirit," and *ology* means "the study of." *Pneumatology* is the study of Holy Spirit. Have you ever studied this topic in Scripture?
- The doctrine of the Trinity is complex. Christianity worships one God in three persons (the Godhead). Christ Jesus, Father God, and Holy Spirit are

fully God and mutually indwell one another. You can't separate Their work, but you can recognize Their roles. How would you describe this concept to a child?

Watch Jenny's Lesson 1 Teaching: The Awe in the Already and Not Yet

URL: davidccook.org/access

Code: Presence

Living Out Theology

- As Jenny mentioned in the video teaching, living in the "already and not yet" tension seems like following squiggles on a map as we journey to our destination. Can you share a time when experiencing unknown peaks or valleys brought you to a deeper understanding of God?
- In the busyness of life, whether you're a student, work professional, mom, grandma, or something in between, how do you maintain the perspective that God's Spirit is with you in the uncertainties and what-ifs?
- This week's reading focuses on words spoken when Holy Spirit was poured out. Acts 2:19 says: "I [God] will show wonders in the heavens above and signs on the earth below." Can you share a time you've experienced God's wonders? In what way did that change you?

Prayer Team

There's power in prayer! Give everyone a piece of paper, or use the Prayer Cards downloaded from jennyrandle.com/presence. If you're comfortable, include your name and/or contact information on the paper, or you can keep this anonymous. Write down your prayer request. This can be for yourself, a family member, a friend, or for your church. Once done, fold the paper and have the group leader randomly pass out the Prayer Cards. Pray over the request you received this week. If the requester included her name, send her some encouragement!

This Week

Read week 1 and answer the corresponding questions.

Week 1

THE WONDER OF GOD'S SPIRIT

*"I will show wonders in the heavens above
and signs on the earth below."*

Acts 2:19

"Jennifer Randle?"

As soon as I said hello to the person on the phone, there was a long pause. She said a lot in between not saying anything at all.

I could hear her taking deep breaths and shuffling her papers on the other side of the phone. It was as if she was stalling to gather her thoughts.

"We have your mammogram results. There are some inconsistencies in our findings, so you'll need to come get an ultrasound at the breast cancer screening center."

There's that word again. *Cancer.* Cancer had been a dangling threat to me for the past three years. My symptoms and follow-up tests had given my medical team some ammo for further scans and biopsies. Every time I went for a medical checkup, I held my breath, waiting for the other shoe to drop. Blood cancer, thyroid cancer, skin cancer, endometrial cancer—the list seemed endless. At lunch with a friend recently, I joked this was what aging must be: a never-ending series of medical tests and mysteries.

Waiting for the test results was torture as I wondered what my future held. My trust in God didn't stop me from turning to Dr. Google, scouring medical websites and forums for information about my symptoms and pending results. I learned to watch for specific markers on my blood tests and to look for red flags on my brain scan. And now, I had a new thing to investigate—breast cancer. If I learned enough, perhaps the confusion surrounding my future doom would stop. *I've since found I was searching for peace in the wrong places.*

All the past tests had returned benign, meaning no cancer, and I am grateful. Yet I couldn't resolve the questions plaguing my friends who have faced different outcomes in their own medical trials. Or the what-ifs within my own.

As the woman on the other end of the line spoke, her voice pulled me back to the present. I was reminded my symptoms remained as her voice momentarily quieted the spinning wheels in my head. "Do you have any questions?" she asked.

I had a lot of questions, but they weren't for her. They were all for God.

Problem

How do we gain God's perspective when the problems seem relentless? First, we must identify our problem. Then instead of wondering why bad things happen, we must search for the beauty of God within them. God certainly isn't the cause of chaos, but gaining His perspective helps us navigate our problems with wisdom, strength, and authority.

In preschool I saw firsthand that a shift in perspective can change everything. At the time I was blindsided by a problem: poor eyesight! I was prescribed glasses, so I picked out an iconic pair with Strawberry Shortcake on the side—pretty sure I was a fashion icon before I even knew that was a thing. As I wore my brand-new glasses for the first time, my steps became unsteady. The ground seemed shaky, and each stride felt like a monumental climb up a giant mountain. My parents each held one of my hands, and the earthquake-ish ground beneath me stabilized. Over time, I got used to this perspective.

Looking through these lenses was strengthening my eyesight. Remember that story as we dive into this week's lessons! We're putting on our godly glasses to see our problems clearer and tackle any uphill battles we may be facing. We're also cleaning our lenses with some metaphorical glass cleaner (thank You, Holy Spirit). Our journey may seem shaky at points, but we hold steady as we're stabilized by God and His perspective.

Pause

To maintain a godly perspective after identifying any problems, we need to remember the art of the dramatic pause.

See what I did there?

The period in the English language concludes a thought, while the question mark pauses for interrogation. Life, in general, can feel like a giant, interrogating question mark. Some say our wondering in life leads to discovering purpose, an existential crisis, or even a quest for spiritual enlightenment. I call the interrogating pause a break from the examination where the breath of God takes up residence. Dramatic, yes. Reality? I think so. Within our human wondering, our pause after a question is a space holder for our natural world to find peace within a supernatural one. **Wherever your wondering may lead you, week 1 of *The Promised Presence* is for those in-between moments where the mystery of life is desperate for an answer.**

As we process through the what-ifs of circumstances yet fully revealed, how do we endure in faith even when facing hard times, doubt, or sorrow? Even when we have what the world would call "our greatest successes," why do we feel unfulfilled and desire more? *Oh, that pesky question mark.* Within the Christian faith, we await Jesus' return as God's kingdom fully reigns on earth as it does in heaven. But how do we wait well?

Pause and Reflect

Just as I had so many questions for God after hearing concerning news, I'm wondering if you might too. Pause and think through what problems in your life are waiting for an answer.

We meet the wonder of God's Spirit as He leads us to repentance, and as we notice His providential care through comfort, help, and guidance. We encounter His power that brings greater freedom, miracles, signs, and wonders. With a deeper understanding of who Holy Spirit is, your own wonder and curiosity will transform from confusion, doubt, or isolation into worship. After all, it's not in your strength you find answers and resolutions, but in God's.

When it comes to God's Spirit, we must also hold space to understand the wonder of the triune God! The path of the Christian faith starts with knowing Jesus as Savior. In salvation when Christ becomes our Savior, God's Spirit indwells us, inviting us into fellowship with Him. Father God promised to send His presence; therefore, you cannot separate Holy Spirit from the work of Father God and Christ Jesus. You can't worship only one-third of the Trinity or compartmentalize Christianity to worship Christ only. After all, they mutually indwell one another. The triune God is worthy to be worshipped and adored. There is such complexity to the conversation!

Let's champion the notion there's more to life than what we see in front of us. We may not always get the answers to our problems that we think are best. *Because, praise the Lord, I didn't marry Joey from New Kids on the Block after I invited him to my middle school birthday party.* I like to think it was the providence of the Lord he apparently never received my love-note invitation.

Seriously, though, the miracles of God are mysterious. Why does He do what He does? God sent a helper through His Spirit. This is a fact. Yet, how come my SOS prayer to the "helpline" hasn't been answered yet? We may not always understand why things end up the way they do, and we may want a different result altogether. Is it possible to become a woman who lets go of her ideal plan and the curated life she thinks she should have? In the questions, can we pause to receive the breath of God? Miracles

> **Theological Term**
>
> **Holy Spirit**—An active presence of God throughout the creation story to the completed story. Christ's followers have been given the gift of a helper who transforms, guides, and empowers them as they endure in faith in a world being redeemed. He is a "he," not an "it." He is not a substance but the third person of the Trinity. He is co-eternal and co-equal to Father God and Lord Jesus.

are unraveling in these mysteries of life, and there's great comfort in being close to the God of Wonder.

Provision

A few days after the call, I went to the breast cancer screening center to deal with the abnormal findings on my mammogram. Having undergone my third back-to-back test, I got dressed. The technician placed her hand on the small of my back, rubbed it, and ushered me out of the room. Her silence and the compassionate rub brought deep restlessness and inner turmoil. Since becoming a Christian, I'd never questioned Jesus as a healer. Yet, as I stepped out of the technician's room at the hospital, I wondered if He would be *my* healer.

I did the thing where I made up fake scenarios. Please tell me I'm not the only one who inadvertently creates a melodramatic movie scene in their head. (Lord, forgive me.) *The slow rub was clearly a sign she knows I am going to die.* I made a mental list of people I would ask to pray over me and lead worship at my hospital bedside. I sat in the waiting room, panicked, and numbed out by watching daytime TV. With one touch, my world was ending.

A crisis of faith is not where my pen is leading the conversation. My faith is the only stabilizing sustenance I have found in the face of eternity. I have faith God is a God of miracles. I know a God who sent angelic visitors to set the prisoners free. I know the One who healed with a touch of the garment. I've sought healing prayers from leaders as they anointed me with oil. Yet when I began to wonder if my wondrous God would intervene for *me*, I'm embarrassed to admit my worry trumped the Word as I let chaos take center stage to His peace. It's strange to feel settled in my soul while spiraling in my mind. *Fix it, Jesus.* Waiting and hoping are close friends, I suppose. I wonder if assumption and disappointment are the evil uncles whispering anxiety-producing lies.

The hospital's inner waiting room was sparse with activity. Women sat in thin paper gowns in a handful of chairs scattered in messy rows. Alone with my thoughts and uncertain anticipation, my brain spiraled as my stomach flip-flopped. My name was called, snapping me out of my inner monologue. I was greeted by a nurse who brought me back to my doctor's office, an empty room with a desk and three chairs. It was like all those movies I watched where they wait to get the results, and then it dissolves into a slow-motion montage of their life eventually fading to black.

My montage daydream started and, a few minutes later, got interrupted by clapping as my doctor walked in.

"All clear!" she said. "It was a cyst, and it resolved itself." She explained a few other things, but it went in one ear and out the other as I slowly exhaled and waited to run as fast as I could through the maze of hospital halls to get to my car. I'm pretty sure it's apparent to all of us that I let the anxiety do the talking in this situation. I'm not proud of that. I'm a woman of faith who knows the Resolver of all things, but in my desperation, I responded so human-like.

Does God need me to respond with my finest moment, or does He just want me to welcome Him? They don't teach you the Ministry of Desperation in seminary or Sunday school. My response in the uncertain and out-of-control moments of wondering was not my finest moment. God is a God of wonder; I know that to be true. He has done and is doing wonderful miracles that bring about redemption, healing, and wholeness. God is a miraculous and very in-control God. Everything is sovereign and under *His* control, and what some call a chance occurrence could be a divine design. As we welcome Holy Spirit, His perspective often becomes ours.

I drove home that day worshipping and thanking God, wondering if I had witnessed a miracle of healing: Was this cyst "resolving itself" actually resolved by God? As I spent time praying days later, a phrase stuck in my mind on repeat. So, I grabbed a note, wrote it down, and stuck it on my computer. Every day at work, I pause to read the pink paper with my scribbly writing. *I know a God who brings dead things back to life.*

This is revival.

This reminds me of the other areas of wondering in my life that feel hopeless and broken. We must take the pause and look for God. He provides. Sometimes, God's provision looks like miraculous intervention; other times, God's provision looks like connecting the dots or bringing comfort and supernatural peace. In our questions, unknowns, and lack of finest moments, hope can always be found in God!

WEEK 1—THE WONDER OF GOD'S SPIRIT

Progress

A miracle will always be mysterious. Our finite brains can't fully comprehend an infinite God. We can hold on to this hope, though: within the pain, purpose is found in God. He is unraveling the most remarkable rescue plan and that is a miracle in itself! We get to live out this mystery of life knowing the Miracle Worker as He moves our story toward completion.

> I know a God who brings dead things back to life. This is revival.

You heard a few of my challenges with uncertain health outcomes and over-dramatized worry. Yet, in the pause of my wondering, I saw a wondrous God working in more ways than one. *God is a God of miracles.* That's not a fluffy line to pacify our pain or to manipulate us to minister pretend miracles within our spaces. Our strength isn't found in knowing the truth that God is miraculous on a theological level. God's strength finds you as your knowledge and chaos collide, and you cry out to a God who is both *with you* and *for you*. He brings provision and comfort.

But what happens when He meets us with a miracle?

This week, we'll examine the miracles in Luke and Acts in depth. We'll discover the miracles were as much for the onlookers as for the individuals who received them. The miracle *always* progressed Jesus' message forward, and goodness followed. We can break down the responses to hundreds of miracle encounters into four categories:

1. The onlookers repented and followed Jesus.
2. The group was struck by fear and amazement at God's power.

3. The witnesses gave God glory and honor and became motivated to serve.
4. Mostly, those who saw could not contain their excitement and told others about the power of Jesus. Sharing their testimony about God's actions intrigued and inspired people to seek out Jesus for themselves.

People sharing their miracle stories was how the gospel spread, the early church started, and today's church still finds strength. When I reflect on the impact of the miracles I encountered in real life and within the biblical text, I know the miracle didn't happen because a perfect prayer was said or enough wishing for wellness was prayed into the abyss. A person did not make the miracle happen. God chose to move a storyline forward in the way He deemed best.

The storyline common to all God's miracles pointed people back to Himself. Theologian Wayne Grudem wrote, "There is nothing inappropriate in seeking miracles for the proper purposes for which they are given by God: to confirm the truthfulness of the gospel message, to bring help to those in need, to remove hindrances to people's ministries, and to bring glory to God."[1]

Jesus' ministry on earth and early church development were built on moments of transformative miracles, and signs and wonders that often led to repentance and a life devoted to Christ. This was how the gospel message went forth. Demons came out of people. People were raised from the dead. Food was multiplied. Angels appeared. And don't forget the greatest miracle of all—the death, resurrection, and ascension of Jesus!

Christ followers are walking out what the Acts church began. I, too, have witnessed miracles like those in the early church. Miracles where God brings about a change of trajectory, providing unexpected results to otherwise expected outcomes. I saw God's provision when a friend received a mystery check to cover his bills while money was tight; God met a woman sick with lupus with physical healing; and a baby born three months early is alive (more on that later).

You may call instances like these coincidences, misdiagnoses, or a positive outcome after forcing down all those vegetables for better health. I believe they are evidence of God's desire to bring His supernatural power into our natural world. These miracles serve as signposts in this journey of faith. However, I can't help but wonder if what we classify as a "miracle" our wondrous God calls a "Monday," as it's just a normal part of who He is.

Spotlight of the Week

Figure 2. Godly Perspective in the Wondering
How God brings calm in a world of confusion

Problem ⟶ Pause ⟶ Provision ⟶ Progress

Problem: Identify the question needing a response
Pause: Create breathing space for the wonder of God
Provision: Receive God's peace, providence, or miraculous intervention
Progress: Praise God for the forward momentum following His provision

Day 1

MYSTERIES OF THE MIRACULOUS

How do I see God's perspective in the unseen plans?

"The holy, mysterious, majestic God, who is not one of us, is willing to come to us, to fill us with the Spirit, and this makes it possible for human beings, who are not God, to know the things of God, to 'discern all things,' to 'have the mind of Christ.'"[2]

Beth Jones, *God the Spirit*

Pray

Holy Spirit, fill me with Your love. Amen.

Read and Study Luke 10:25–28

Life is out of control. Or shall I say, life often feels out of our control, even for those with organized sock drawers and big-bucks bank accounts. As I write this, a coworker's child struggles with suicidal thoughts, a relationship on the rocks seems desperate for resolution, and a friend with debilitating mental health issues lost the ability to function in her job.

We each have a list of concerns. For some women, the list of questions hits in the midnight hour. The interrogating pause plagues us as we're trying to drift off to sleep. How do we maintain a healthy perspective when life feels so confusing and chaotic? How has God equipped and empowered us to live with hope in a world of hurt? *This* question mark creates a cross-examination of a soul longing to see God finish what He started.

Christ followers live in what theologians call "the already and not yet"—a tension between the present reality and the promised kingdom to come. In the already, God has won the victory over sin and death when Jesus died and rose again, but it's not yet the fullness of victory, which will one day be revealed to us at His second coming within new creation.

Living in this "already and not yet" feels like squiggles on a map as we head to the finish line, our final destination where we're united with God face to face. This truth is our eschatological hope, our end-time hope in a world becoming beautiful. But how can we find comfort and certainty in the right now as we journey toward the ultimate restoration?

Our faith is stable but rarely straightforward. In the context of our faith journeys, let's think through the word *wonder*. We're going to need some wonder as we tackle the mysterious in our world. Wonder can take a few forms:

- Wonder (verb): The wonder of a person is simply when we have questions or are curious. For example, "I wonder why I'm still single?" Or "I wonder why my kid didn't get into that school?" Or "I wonder how God created each snowflake to be unique?"
- Wondrous (adjective): The term *wondrous* describes an attribute of God, highlighting His extraordinary nature. For example, God is wondrous as He performs miracles beyond our comprehension and creates beautiful things.
- Wonderment (noun): Wonderment is a state of awe prompted by encountering the divine qualities and actions of God. His magnificence and glory evoke a sense of wonder and awe in those who experience it. For example, wonderment is displayed as we encounter God's presence in a tangible way.

When these three forms of wonder converge, our questions meet the wondrous God and we're left in awe. The path of the Christ-centered life affords us these moments that mark our journey, ensuring we're headed in the right direction. The convergence of wonder is when we connect with God and are stabilized by Him, making the squiggly path of life feel straight.

Figure 3. Stability in the Waiting and Wondering

The transformation that occurs when human uncertainty converges with God

My Wondering	⇄	**Wondrous God**
Questionable, unstable, always changing, limited in power, and lacking knowledge		Absolute, stable, never changing, all powerful, and all knowing

As the wondrous God meets my wondering, He stabilizes my instability.
As my wondering meets the wondrous God, I respond in wonderment by the unexplainable occurrence.
Both of these responses lead to worship.

The Bible is filled with stories of individuals who faced periods of wondering and intense waiting. Sarah struggled with infertility, wondering when she'd have a child. Mary Magdalene was tormented by demons and in search of freedom. A woman who hosted church fervently prayed for Peter's release from prison. To see how God ended their waiting and wondering, check out their miracles in Genesis 21:1–3, Luke 8:2, and Acts 12:1–17.

We're living a supernatural life in a natural world as we wrestle within the in-between places. Luke wrote of a time when a lawyer tried to test Jesus by asking, "What shall I do to inherit eternal life?" Jesus responded by asking him to answer.

The man responded by quoting Deuteronomy 6:5, "You shall love the Lord your God with all your heart and with all your soul and with all your strength and with all your mind, and your neighbor as yourself."

And Jesus said, "You have answered correctly; do this, and you will live" (Luke 10:25–28). Keep those words at the forefront of your mind as we maintain a godly perspective within the mysteries of living.

On the squiggly path of life, the roadblock with the blazing question mark remains. Triune God, in His all-powerfulness, can swoop in and bring resolve to all the things. *Yet, where is He?* And what do we do in the waiting? How does a miraculous God collide with my meaningful yet sometimes-it-feels-mundane life? Can He be trusted?

These are loaded and deep questions, where answers unveil themselves within the depths of a loving God. *Love the Lord your God with all your heart, soul, strength, and mind (Luke 10:27).* Everything will flow from this—this perspective will help us maintain a healthy theology as Holy Spirit empowers us to persevere in the unknown.

Within the study of Luke–Acts, we see some mysteries unravel as God responds with miracles. And as you wait for your unraveling, even if your questions for God hurt or bring up deep pain, God will provide hope. He is worthy to be trusted. Through the power of God's Spirit, you will endure.

> **Theological Terms**
>
> **Miracle**—A divine act by God where a supernatural experience overrides the natural world.
>
> **Signs and Wonders**—Refers to supernatural events or miracles executed by God or people under God's power. Examples of signs and wonders in the Bible are healing the sick, casting out demons, raising the dead, and creative miracles.

Question

In what ways have you personally seen the wonderment of God stabilize a chaotic or confusing situation? List out those key character traits of God. Hold on to these truths as you continue to love the Lord your God with all your heart, soul, strength, and mind.

Day 2

MIRACLES IN LUKE

Where is Holy Spirit's involvement in Jesus' earthly ministry?

"Christianity is not in essence a moral code or an ascetic routine, as so many down the centuries have mistakenly supposed. Rather, it is a supernaturalizing personal relationship with a supernatural personal Savior."[3]

J. I. Packer and Gary A. Parrett, *Grounded in the Gospel*

Pray

Holy Spirit, thank You for always redirecting my attention to Jesus. Amen.

Read and Study Luke 3:21–22

In the gospel of Luke, we find accounts of ordinary people like you and me who had miraculous experiences. These miracles brought freedom to the recipients, deliverance from demons, salvation, physical and mental healing, and restoration to their communities. We also see creative miracles in nature and providential care. Luke's gospel accounts share more miracles than the other accounts. It's also interesting to note his miracle accounts contain medical terminology the other gospels don't.

Today we'll look at the miracles throughout Jesus' earthly ministry, which lasted around three years. Although we could focus on the miraculous birth of Christ, we'll start at the beginning of Jesus' ministry, after John the Baptist baptized Him. This wasn't the first water baptism, as John had been preaching for people to repent and be baptized. However, this *was* the first baptism of the Spirit; this was a significant moment. As Jesus came up from the water, Holy Spirit descended on Him. Jesus was revealed as God's eternal and unique Son, and Holy Spirit validated His identity (Luke 3:21–22).

The "Wonder List in the Gospel of Luke" (figure 4) lists a variety of problems that meet the amazing wonder of God's Spirit—problems that are resolved with God's out-of-this-world, unexplainable intervention. In these biblical accounts, the people were humble and vulnerable in recognizing they or another person needed help. Their stories reveal brokenness and a desire for resolution. Many of these people paused to seek out Jesus for restoration in their lives. It is the same for you and me—whether you are a working woman, caring for aging parents, dating that hot dude you saw in the church choir, leading in your community, or serving your local church. In the complexities of life, we're bound to approach our all-powerful and all-knowing God with vulnerability in need of solutions.

God is a miracle worker, and it's within His sovereign reign to move as He sees fit. For the thirty-two miracle accounts listed in Luke, their questions were answered by a wondrous God. He healed whole crowds of people and multiplied food for thousands. God showcased His power and might over isolation, sickness, strongholds, and even death. As you establish your theology surrounding miracles, note that these encounters may have brought provision for individuals, but remember these miracles were always more than that. These miracles progressed the message of Christ further, causing many to respond in awe and to live for Him.

Figure 4. Wonder List in the Gospel of Luke

Documented miracles in Luke after Jesus' baptism

Problem	Provision through Miracles	Problem	Provision through Miracles
Demonized; against Jesus	Deliverance (4:31–37)	Diseased crowds	Physical healing (9:11)
Sick mother-in-law	Physical healing (4:39)	5,000 hungry	Providential care (9:13–17)
Diseased crowds	Physical healing; deliverance (4:40–41)	Doubt	Multiple miracles: creative; judgment/rebuke (9:28–36)
Lack of resources at job	Providential care; salvation (5:1–11)	Boy possessed by demon	Deliverance; physical healing (9:37–43)
Leprosy; outcast	Physical healing; social healing (5:12–16)	Division	Social healing (9:49–50)
Paralyzed; against Jesus	Spiritual healing; physical healing (5:17–26)	Wrong focus; demonized	Judgment/rebuke; deliverance (10:17–20)
Withered hand; against Jesus	Physical healing (6:6–11)	Demonized	Deliverance (11:14)
Unclean spirits; diseased	Physical healing; deliverance (6:17–19)	Long-term disability	Physical healing; deliverance (13:10–17)
Facing death	Physical healing (7:1–10)	Dropsy; against Jesus	Physical healing; judgment/rebuke (14:1–4)
Son died; social and financial concerns	Healing from death (resurrection); social healing; providential care (7:11–17)	Ten with leprosy	Physical healing; salvation; social healing (17:11–19)
Evil spirits; diseased; plagued; lack assurance in faith	Physical healing; deliverance; salvation; healing from death (resurrection); judgment/rebuke (7:18–23)	Blind	Physical healing; salvation (18:35–43)

Problem	Provision through Miracles	Problem	Provision through Miracles
Need healing	Physical healing; deliverance (8:1-3)	Ear cut off; violence	Physical healing; judgment/rebuke (22:50-51)
Harsh windstorm	Providential care (8:22-25)	Jesus' crucifixion; darkness at day	Judgment; nature (23:44-49)
Violent; no home; seized by demons	Deliverance; mental healing; social healing (was isolated); salvation (8:26-39)	Tomb was empty	Healing from death (resurrection); salvation for all who believe Jesus' life, death, and resurrection made a way for eternal life (24:4-12)
Woman with the issue of blood	Physical healing; social healing (8:43-48)	Resurrected Jesus not recognized	Creative (24:13-35)
Daughter died	Healing from death (resurrection) (8:49-56)	Resurrected Jesus appears; people frightened	Creative (24:36-52)

For an even more robust chart detailing Luke's theology of miracles in Luke and Acts, visit jennyrandle.com/presence.

Questions

1. How do you see the triune God represented in Luke 3:21–22?

2. What types of miracles are highlighted in Luke?

3. Pick two scriptures referenced in the preceding chart (figure 4). Using the following chart, list the verses (which I call "power grid"—we'll get into that later) and describe the problem; the pause where God showed up; the provision with His peace, providence, or miraculous intervention; and how the message of Christ progressed.

Power Grid	Problem ⟶	Pause ⟶	Provision ⟶	Progress ⟶
Luke 7:11–17	A widowed mother's only son died. In their culture, no male figure in the household had social and financial impact for the widow.	Jesus approached—He saw the widow and had compassion for her.	Multiple miracles: healing from death (resurrection); social healing; provision.	Jesus gave the son back to his mother. The crowds were fearful and glorified God. Reports about Jesus spread through Judea and all the surrounding country.

4. What was the role of Holy Spirit within these miracle encounters?

5. Review the "progress" results and jot down what good followed God's provision. Say a prayer of thanks for a God who moves the story forward!

Day 3

MY WONDER LIST

How can I sustain a sense of wonder if I'm overwhelmed?

"Theology is not primarily the repeating of confessional assertions but, rather, the investigation and clarification of the internal consistency of those assertions, their reasoning about their ground, and the way they relate to the problems of daily life."[4]

Thomas C. Oden, *Classic Christianity*

Pray

Holy Spirit, guide me closer to You. Amen.

Read and Study Luke 1:46–55

There are only so many times I can ask my teenage son, Max, to put his socks in the hamper before I micromanage the mess myself. Like, why are there dirty socks behind the couch cushions, on the hallway counter, and trailing into Max's bedroom? *Fix it, Jesus!* I'm totally over-spiritualizing the moment, but my goodness, how many times do we find ourselves

Context Is Key

Luke 1:26–38 is the account of the angelic visitation with Mary. The angel said, "The Holy Spirit will come upon you, and the power of the Most High will overshadow you; therefore the child to be born will be called holy—the Son of God" (v. 35). Mary learned she was going to play a part in the miraculous birth of the Messiah, which had been foretold (Isa. 7:14). Mary later responded with a song of praise that has become known as "The Magnificat."

taking on the responsibility of cleaning up messes that weren't in our jurisdiction in the first place?

Even as we live for God, it's easy to inadvertently divert our attention from Him as we attempt to reclaim some of the control. We try to troubleshoot this life and the lives of those around us within our own strength. Yes, we've been entrusted to steward our one precious life well, and the ground our feet may touch (Gen. 2:15). But *when* are we crossing the line to taking back control of situations out of our control?

Plenty of areas shape our lives—I call them the "Pillars of Personhood." Consider what pillars God has you focusing on in this stage of your life. Do you need direction or have concerns about any of these pillars? Circle the area(s) you are giving focused attention to currently.

Figure 5. Pillars of Personhood

Nine areas of focus for a purposeful life

Spiritual	Calling	Family	Volunteer Work	Personal Growth
Professional Development	Relationships	Financial	Physical/ Mental Health	Other _____

In understanding the areas God is inviting you to focus your attention, you may discover you have specific questions and burdens surrounding those areas. If you find you're trying to control all the things, take a break before you have a breakdown yourself! Here are three different ways you can pause to see the awe of God in the middle of your overwhelm—or other people's "dirty laundry."

The first pause is one of surrender. When you can stop spinning out of control long enough to position your feet on solid ground, you'll be able to yield control. I get it, though; some of us act like control freaks because organizational skills and getting stuff done are smiled-upon traits that help tackle the real-life to-do list. Who needs sleep (or sanity) when we can micromanage all the things, or stay up late making lists of all the miracles in Luke, to muster up the faith to believe for one too? With a death grip on the results, we weasel our way into finding solutions by intervening, discovering answers with excessive research, or forcing a position on the fast track because we're getting highly impatient. If this sounds like you, pause and relinquish control.

The second type of pause is to assess the situation by slowing down and getting real! We think if we fake a clean house, we belong. We hide the trauma under the bed because we're busy and distracted, and facing the mess requires a gutsy vulnerability that rarely feels safe. After all, if we have a "tidy world void of messes," we'll be that model woman who memorizes the book of Numbers, runs a part-time business that generates six figures, and has family members who put their socks away. However, when we fake a tidy life with a death grip on *our* optimal outcomes, we begin to play a role we were never meant to play—God.

Your life isn't a performance. It is a story of purpose under God's penmanship. The thing preventing women from experiencing closeness with God and His people is the idea that we must keep up an appearance. We have it all together. We can fix it, do it, make it, bake it, tie it in a bow, and fake it until we *make it*.

What does God require of us when it feels like our world is unraveling and we've been in hiding? *Pause.* All God wants is simply us and our reverence. From this posture of desperation and vulnerability, we worship the One worthy of worship.

The third pause is to go to God. We must run to God rather than running away from Him. **Pour out your weakness before a wondrous God.** God already knows, anyway. What if we relinquish control of our ordinary life and rely on God for the extraordinary? What if we trust Him to fill in the gaps of the unknown and to calm situations out of our control? In exchanging the "Why, God?" for "Where are You?" the focus shifts from questioning Him to locating Him.

I've also found the wonder of God as I go into His creation. Go for a walk, see the sunset, or watch the birds from your window. As you take these pause breaks, may you encounter

God's wonder within your wondering this week as you slow down and surrender control, get real, and approach a God who is close. Amen!

Questions

1. In Mary's song in Luke 1:46–55, what key character traits do you notice about God? How do these apply to today's lesson?

2. For the remainder of these questions you'll be creating your own "Wonder List" using figure 6 on the following page. Use this as a prayer tool to pause and see God. Problem: Review the different "Pillars of Personhood" in your life. Whether you're striving or struggling, write down your concerns on the chart. Do you feel out of control or under control? If the problem is in your attempts at control, pray for godly wisdom on what to do next. If it's out of control, pray for God's provision or power to invade your circumstance.

3. Pause: This is the interrogating pause where we take a break and create space to receive the breath of God's wonder within our questions. Obviously, we trust God as the miracle worker in our situation. He can also minister through others to bring about solutions. Has God placed a person within your life to encourage you during this time? Did you hear a sermon from your church that felt like a direct download from heaven? Has Holy Spirit given you direction? Write down the tools God uses to bring provision within those problems.

4. Provision: Keep this chart handy, and over time, note how God explicitly answers your prayers and brings about resolution through supernatural peace, His daily providence, or miraculous intervention.

5. Progress: Reviewing the biblical miracles from Luke and Acts (on pages 47–48 and 59–60) shows transformation within individuals. People grew closer to God, were healed, strengthened, and sustained the church. Consider the lasting fruit and good things following God's provision. This may be days, months, or even years later!

Figure 6. Wonder List in My Life

Documented miracles unfolding in my story

As you process through the list, remember those key character traits of God you listed in question 1. Regardless of circumstance, He is always worthy of our worship.

Problem ⟶ My question needing a response	Pause ⟶ Breathing space for the wonder of God	Provision ⟶ God's peace, providence, or miraculous intervention	Progress Forward momentum following God's provision

Day 4

MIGHTY ACTS

How are ordinary believers empowered to do extraordinary things?

"Only the Holy Spirit ignites faith, transforming human effort into holy fire that comes roaring into our lives at the first hint of welcome, insistent on igniting us, sharing us, and being shared."[5]
Kenda Creasy Dean, *Almost Christian*

Pray

Holy Spirit, thank You for empowering the church. Amen.

Read and Study Acts 2:2–13

Use me, God. I beg to be used by You so I can find solace outside myself. I am out of words. The pen stops writing. The story pauses in an uncomfortable silence as this right-now beautifully broken situation reeks of injustice. My storyline stays still just enough to get caught up in Yours. Yours is a story of redemption. Let me see it. You minister in my desperation with comfort, peace, and a reminder that there's more to life than what's in front of me. You are working and I want to move with You. This pain sends me into a fetal position at Your feet. Carry me. I wrote those words during prayer after another disappointment.

When life becomes heavy, it can feel hard to do the everyday things like making dinner, responding to work emails, or hitting up the gym. Yet, we're women who show up anyway. So, in the tenderhearted place I found myself within hard circumstances outside my control, I continued my ministry schedule as the Lord willed it and after seeking advice from my pastor.

I'll never forget a woman I met at an event I was speaking at. After teaching, I invited anyone forward who had been playing pretend, acting like everything was fine, but in reality, they were struggling. Women lined up at the altar.

Joy was the first person I reached my hand out to pray with. Almost immediately, she was overwhelmed by God's power and fell to the ground. This wasn't an everyday occurrence for me, so I awkwardly said out loud, "Oh, okay, Lord, we're doing this." For some reason, on this day, God changed Joy's story. Even in my own desperation, Holy Spirit ministered hope through me anyway.

Weeks later, Joy and I connected. She told me that she had been faking fine for years and had been in a dark and lonely place. Joy said she tangibly felt the power of God go out from me and onto her. She knew she was healed at that altar, and she shared how God had brought her joy back after years of deep depression.

To have people testify to encountering a miracle from God blows me away every time. I stand in awe at the greatness of who He is. This isn't new, though. All throughout Scripture, we see the proclamation of the gospel and signs and wonders go hand in hand. This is a biblical model. It goes way back through generations of church history and continues into our modern-day church.

The book of Acts shares the establishment of the early church. It's where we see Holy Spirit poured out on God's people. Ordinary disciples are filled with the extraordinary power of God's Spirit. We read about Holy Spirit filling Peter (Acts 2:2–4), Stephen (6:5), and Paul (9:12–17). Other people God used as conduits of His miracle-working power are Philip and Ananias, although the Bible doesn't specifically tell us when Holy Spirit came upon them. As Christ's mission relocated from a physical one on earth to ascending into heaven at the right hand of the Father (7:55–56), He made way for the gospel to continue to go to the ends of the earth (1:4–11). **If you take time to study all the miracles in Acts, you'll find that one cannot systemize the** supernatural or manipulate a move of God. You can simply witness a miraculous God on the move … and dare to participate if He's given you the tenacity too.

Figure 7. Wonder List in the Book of Acts
Documented miracles in Acts

Problem	Provision through Miracles	Problem	Provision through Miracles
Disciples wonder about kingdom restoration	Creative: signs/wonders (1:4–11)	Salvation only for the Jews	Creative: communication (10:1–7)
Disciples wait for the promised Spirit to come	Manifestations of the Spirit: speaking in tongues (2:2–13)	Disunity between Jews and Gentiles	Creative: communication; salvation; manifestation of the Spirit: speaking in tongues (10:9–43)
Faith in Christ needed to continue to be taught	Signs and wonders; salvation; providential care (2:42–47)	Peter in prison; church praying for release	Creative: providence; social healing (12:6–16)
Lame from birth	Physical healing (3:2–10)	Prideful king	Judgment (12:24–25)
Lied to Holy Spirit	Judgment (5:3–11)	False prophet	Judgment/rebuke (13:9–12)
Many sick; unclean spirits	Signs and wonders; physical healing; deliverance; salvation (5:12–16)	Unbelieving Jews poisoned the minds of Gentile believers	Signs and wonders (14:1–7)
Apostles arrested	Providential care (5:18–21)	Crippled person; idol worship	Physical healing; judgment/rebuke (14:8–18)

Problem	Provision through Miracles	Problem	Provision through Miracles
Against apostle; falsely accused	Signs and wonders; rebuke (6:8–7:60)	Fortune teller enslaved	Deliverance (16:16–24)
Persecution against the church	Deliverance; physical healing; salvation (8:4–8)	Paul and Silas in prison	Providential care (16:25–40)
Difficulty understanding Scripture	Manifestations of the Spirit: word of knowledge; salvation; creative (8:26–40)	Illegitimate faith; magic	Physical healing; deliverance; spiritual healing (19:11–20)
Saul persecutes Christians	Creative: miraculous appearance; rebuke; communication (9:1–16)	Fell from a third floor and died	Healing from death (resurrection) (20:9–12)
Saul is blind	Physical healing; salvation (9:17–22)	Severe storm	Creative: provision (27:21–44)
Paralyzed; bedridden	Physical healing; salvation (9:33–35)	Deadly snake bite	Physical healing (28:3–6)
Ill; died	Healing from death (resurrection); salvation (9:36–41)	Fever; dysentery	Physical healing (28:7–10)

In Acts 4:23–31, after John and Peter were threatened and released, they went and chatted with their friends, sharing what the council had said. They turned to prayer and praised God for who He is, then they petitioned God for three things. First, in the midst of threats, would

God keep them in mind. Two, would God enable His servants to speak with great boldness. Lastly, would God stretch out His hand and bring healing. Ladies, let this be the cry of our hearts. This is the Acts way!

I heard a theologian teach that the remedy for lukewarmness is Holy Spirit.[6] Christ followers were given a promised helper who turned ordinary people into Spirit-filled miracle workers. This is how believers continue to live on mission as Holy Spirit ministers miracles, signs, and wonders through them to the world around them. God's Spirit is the active agent the global church needs to stay alive and purified. Within the concerns of our modern-day living and the intercession for the lukewarm church, Holy Spirit empowers His people to respond within the pause and to receive the breath of life. What would it look like if you believed that to be true?

> Christ followers were given a promised helper who turned ordinary people into Spirit-filled miracle workers.

Questions

1. In Acts 2:2–13 how is Holy Spirit connected to the ministry of the apostles? What does this say about the character of God?

2. What types of miracles are highlighted in Acts?

3. Pick two scriptures referenced in the "Wonder List in the Book of Acts" in figure 7. Using the following chart, list the verses (power grid), describe the problem, the pause where God showed up, the provision with His peace, providence, or miraculous intervention, and how the message of Christ progressed after the miracle.

Power Grid	Problem →	Pause →	Provision →	Progress
Acts 8:4–8	Persecution against the church.	Philip went to Samaria and proclaimed Christ and performed miracles.	Multiple fixes: deliverance; physical healing; salvation.	The gospel went forth; many people were physically healed and freed from unclean spirits; joy in the city.

4. What's the role of Holy Spirit within these miracle encounters?

5. Looking back at how you completed the "pause" column, who did God minister through? How does this empower you to minister within your own faith journey?

Day 5

MIRACLES IN LIFE AND DEATH

What does God's provision look like in pain?

"Even when life is out of control, God is in control, and my only response was to trust Him."[7]

Carol Marsella, my mom

> This lesson shares a story of infant loss.
> Please proceed with sensitivity if needed.

Pray

Holy Spirit, thank You for Your comfort. Amen.

Read and Study Acts 12:5–17

The Bible lists hundreds of miraculous stories from the Old Testament to the New Testament. We read of moments when God invades everyday life with miracles. My theology believes Jesus is the same yesterday, today, and forever (Heb. 13:8), so I believe in miracles in the present day too. *But I wasn't always that way.*

In elementary school, I attended religious education within the Catholic Church. I vividly recall a lesson where the classroom was adorned with candles, soft music, and throw pillows.

Even my sixth-grade self could appreciate the beauty of the atmosphere. As we delved into the study, the director wondered, "Have you ever witnessed a miracle?" I quickly responded no, and the lesson continued.

But as I reflected on this experience later with my parents, Mom said, "You are a miracle." At twenty-seven weeks pregnant with me—her second child—my mom was bleeding and dilated so she was sent into the hospital and put on bedrest. If born too soon, I could have had major lung difficulties, which could have led to brain trauma. At the time, babies born at twenty-seven weeks' gestation were on the verge of surviving. Their medical treatment could make the difference between life and death.

"You were right on the cusp of living or dying. This was the first time I had to truly trust God. I had nothing else I could do. I knew if you lived, He would have big plans for your life," Mom said.

"You were born a few weeks later. Your cries were faint and feeble, resembling the sound of a little battery-operated doll. You weighed 1 pound, 12 ounces and were immediately rushed to the NICU." It was God's providential care I was at a state-of-the-art neonatal intensive care unit where babies from surrounding areas were sent for the highest level of care.

"When your mom and I could finally go in to see you, someone called the priest to give you your last rights. Priests do this for people who are in great danger of dying. So, being the athletic football guy I was, I stood between you in the incubator and the priest. Pushing him, I yelled, 'You're not getting over here!'" My dad's voice was strong as he continued. "I just knew if I could touch you, I could give you strength. And as I reached out to touch your hand, you grabbed my finger instead. I was the one empowered to go on."

"You stayed in the hospital for three months after I was released. One day during dinner, we got a call, and they told us after doing an X-ray, they saw bleeding in your brain," Mom said.

Dad continued, "The doctors told us chances of survival were very little. Your Nonna [my dad's mom] called all her nun friends and started the prayer chains."

"By the time we showed up at the hospital, they had rerun the test, and nothing was there. It was a clear brain scan. Perhaps a lab error, maybe an answered prayer. It was a rollercoaster of emotions day after day. After months in the hospital, you came home weighing 4 pounds, 5 ounces," Mom said. "My whole life, I thought I had control. Look at us; we have great jobs and a wonderful family. Then something like this happens, and you realize you don't have control over so many things. I felt the presence of God all over the NICU! Your dad had more faith than me; he knew you would be fine."

It was different for my sister, Nicole, born three years later at thirty-four weeks' gestation with a diaphragmatic hernia (a life-threatening congenital disability). As soon as she was delivered, Nicole immediately went into surgery. Eleven hours later, my parents said their goodbyes, and she died in my mom's arms.

The miracle wasn't in her death but in the life God brought after. During Nicole's birth and mine, in both life and death, the power of God made a way when it seemed there was none. A life sustained, a marriage persevered, loving family support in trials, the list goes on. In both circumstances, there was the closeness of a miraculous God.

The morning after Nicole died, my dad, exhausted and lost, ran into his boss's daughter, a nurse, in the hospital elevator. She helped him and called her father, who supported our family tremendously. My mom worked through her grief and did not wave a finger at God. Instead, she had faith that light was waiting to come from the dark, which led to my baby brother. Profound grief from death and the difficulty within my birth story led to overwhelming gratitude and a perspective shift. My mom shared how these hardships were deeply impactful in growing her faith too.

This is the already-and-not-yet tension of this life.

We're not called to rescue ourselves or be perfect; we're called to acknowledge the One who *is* the perfect rescuer. **God brings stability within the instability of humanity.** This is when the squiggly path of life feels straight as we connect with an ever-present God. He makes our paths straight as these uncertainties untangle and find resolution in Him. Humility is the posture to take for the miraculous to take place.

Miracles are for today and can be found in both life's mighty and mundane moments. We don't build our faith around chasing miracles; they are simply byproducts of a miraculous God. There is so much more to our faith than the eyes can see.

> We're not called to rescue ourselves or be perfect; we're called to acknowledge the One who *is* the perfect rescuer.

There's a verse in Proverbs that says, "Trust in the LORD with all your heart, and do not lean on your own understanding. In all your ways acknowledge him, and he will make straight your paths" (3:5–6). The Christian faith affords us stability in a rarely straightforward life. In Christ, our circumstances find a cushion of security to land. These question marks in life leave us leaning into the One with all the answers. Our humanity may be breakable, but our loving God is able.

Questions

1. In Acts 12:5–17 how did God bring stability within Peter's instability?

2. How did Mary's prayer gathering play an instrumental role in Peter's rescue?

3. What was their response to Peter's miracle (v. 16)?

4. In the story of my parents, how do you see God's provision within the different circumstances of their daughters' birth outcomes? How can reflecting on this help you in your own journey?

5. God loves you! Continue to maintain this godly perspective. Take time to pause and write out a prayer focusing on our wondrous God. Invite Holy Spirit into your prayer time as you reflect on all you learned about His character this week.

BENEDICTION

"May the God of hope fill you with all joy and peace as you trust in him, so that you may overflow with hope by the power of the Holy Spirit" (Rom. 15:13 NIV).

WEEK 2 PRE-SESSION QUESTIONS AND TEACHING VIDEO

Community Connection

Start off the discussion by sharing some "Yay God" praiseworthy moments from the week. Taking time to celebrate how you see God moving is pivotal in recognizing a God on the move.

Learning Theology

- This past week, we read about the Wonder of God's Spirit. Our "Spotlight" was on how to maintain a godly perspective in the wondering and waiting. What stood out to you in this week's lesson regarding Holy Spirit?
- See pages 47–48, 59–60, or 49 and 61, question 3. Miracles propelled the gospel forward. In reviewing more than fifty miracle accounts found throughout Luke and Acts, we see people responded to miracles in four ways: They would repent and follow Jesus, be amazed, serve, and testify to His power. How specifically did you see that to be true in Luke and Acts?

- See pages 50 and 62, question 4. How did the Holy Spirit empower the apostles and early Christians?

Watch Jenny's Lesson 2 Teaching: The Unseen Life

URL: davidccook.org/access

Code: Presence

Living Out Theology

- Even though something seems unseen, it can still carry an impact that is seen. As Jenny taught about God's organizational chart, how specifically have you seen Holy Spirit act as your rudder guiding you toward God?
- Knowing a personal God is leading you toward an abundant life, how does that impact your daily decisions and habits?
- This week's reading focuses on Jesus' words in Luke 24:49: "Behold, I am sending the promise of my Father upon you …" In thinking about God being a Promise Keeper, how do those words bring comfort?

Prayer Team

See figure 6 ("Wonder List in My Life") on page 55. Is there something on your Wonder List we can pray for? Grab a Prayer Card and write it down. Once done, fold the paper and have the group leader randomly pass out the cards. Pray over the request you received this week. If you're able, send some encouragement to the person you're praying for!

This Week

Read week 2 and answer the corresponding questions.

Week 2

THE PRESENT REALITY OF GOD'S SPIRIT

"Behold, I am sending the promise of my Father upon you."
Luke 24:49

"Are we doing this right?" My voice hushed over the phone to my pastor as Ashley leaned in for his response.

As we huddled in the corner of the bathroom, the gravity of the situation was not lost on me—we were in hiding, sketching out a battle plan against a demon. We had prayed for more than an hour, but we still had a long road ahead.

It was the spring of 2022. I was out of town at an interdenominational Christian event hosted by my friend and church leader, Ashley, who had invited me to speak and minister.

When I'd woken up that morning, I'd felt a deep comfort and knowing I couldn't quite put into words. I can only describe this as a moment with God. His voice wasn't audible, but I recognized Holy Spirit as close. It felt as if He had said, **"You've been tiptoeing, but I've set your feet to run. You've been in training; it's time to go. There's a grid for this. There's a grid for this. There's a grid for this."**

I didn't have enough life skills to pump myself up with such talk before 7:00 a.m., or coffee, and I knew the repetitive phrase couldn't be ignored. I had better figure out this grid and fast! Little did I know this was the beginning of the preparation leading us to face a radical move of God's Spirit later that day.

The Grid

> **Theological Term**
> Pneumatology—The study of Holy Spirit.

Let's imagine God's Word like a power grid. Power grids do three things—make the power system reliable, secure best practices for the energy, and produce a greater capacity for power. The Bible is reliable and trustworthy regarding who God is and His character. The Bible guides us with best practices by providing boundaries and wisdom toward God's will that helps us live godly lives. The Bible provides power as Holy Spirit gives strength and gifts to Christ followers by ministering through them within the boundaries of Scripture.

As Christians, our power grid (or grid) is the Bible giving us a biblical worldview centered on God. The living Word of God (Heb. 4:12) provides our battle plan, boundaries, and most importantly, intimacy with the main character and author of the story, triune God. Keeping the Bible in the proper context in which it was written helps us process God's supernatural move in the natural world. It's essential to view Scripture as sacred, the absolute truth of God, and a source of power!

Within this grid are some nonnegotiables in the Christian faith. Some refer to these as the first-tier essentials, or the truths relating to salvation in Christianity.

Some of these include:
- the centrality of Christ as the only Lord and Savior
- the death and resurrection of Jesus
- humanity's sinful nature and the need for a Savior
- the doctrine of the Trinity
- the second coming of Christ

My goal in this study is to teach truths regarding the doctrine of Holy Spirit, specifically around His transforming power and authority. This will inform how we receive and respond to God's Spirit.

We agree on the foundations. Christ is risen and He is Lord! If we disagree about the workings of Holy Spirit's power, we're still in agreement on the essentials of the Christian faith. So we're not in a battle; in fact, we're on the same team and united because of Christ. Study the grid and biblical boundaries for yourself, and trust Holy Spirit to help you and discover more of Him.

As we understand the biblical grid, we become women who rely on God's Spirit to walk in powerful authority and produce godly fruit. Our godly attributes must be a cosigner to God's spiritual gifts ministering through us. Both godly fruit and godly power are markers of genuine faith. Looking at Jesus' earthly ministry, we can see He helped those demonized and sick, and He was filled with love and compassion for the hurting. As we seek to embrace Holy Spirit in a confused and hurting world, I want us to sit together through these pages and prayerfully look to God.

The author of Luke and Acts is Luke, who's been referred to as "the theologian of the Holy Spirit" because God's Spirit is prominent in his writings.[1] Understanding who wrote the gospel of Luke and Acts, the time frame, and the cultural context of the era is critical to understanding the biblical grid. (See figure 1 on page 21 for a quick understanding of both books!) Keeping in mind the proper background of the books will help you best interpret Scripture around pneumatology while equipping you to realize what that means for the present-day believer.

> **Looking at Jesus' earthly ministry, we can see He helped those demonized and sick, and He was filled with love and compassion for the hurting.**

Biblical accounts aren't written from the perspective of our modern-day society but in a much different time frame than in our Westernized world. If you want to go deeper in a story, study the surrounding scriptures of our daily passages to get a fuller picture. Make it a point to understand the context fully by grasping what the text says about God's character and how Jesus fits into the storyline, then prayerfully consider how this applies to your modern-day living. As you read the Bible, always keep God first!

The Training

Alongside the power grid of Scripture, God so graciously reminded me I had been in training—and so have you. I'm not a PhD candidate and have skipped over the book of Leviticus more times than I'd like to admit. I'm a normal gal who occasionally wears socks and sandals while crying in parking lots because I wasn't invited to the party. It just so happens I get to write words within my wonderment as I experience some adventurous things with God.

As I've ministered around the world across denominational lines, I've learned we tend to gravitate toward different ways of spiritual formation. This can result in specific theological leanings (good or bad). In short, we have assumptions about God and Christianity based on our history. Here's *my* background. I was raised Catholic in my formative years of childhood. I entered Christianity through a Pentecostal church, where I became a born-again believer at eighteen. I attended a variety of churches for a while. My family currently attends a Bible-teaching church that recognizes the supernatural gifts yet expresses them conservatively.

To overly simplify the impact of each:
- The nondenominational churches taught me about servant leadership and that the church can be creative.
- The reformed Calvinists taught me how to study the Bible and how God's Word catalyzes transformation.
- The Pentecostals taught me about God's power and gifts.
- The Baptists taught me the importance of preserving the truth of Scripture and gathering with a church family.

In my faith journey, I've seen God minister signs and wonders in both demonstrative, charismatic settings and traditional liturgical spaces. Witnessing God's power in various settings has taught me so much about Him, and I'm left humbled in awe every single time God meets His people in a tangible way.

The formal side of my religious training was in a graduate school at a seminary rooted in the Wesleyan movement. I've studied the historical roots of the charismatic belief in a variety of denominations from the age of the martyrs and within the nineteenth century to the present day.

I found myself involved in media ministry at eighteen when I learned it was a thing. In my twenties, I worked in part-time ministry in a variety of positions: volunteered in a youth group; produced a local Christian TV show; coordinated services at a megachurch, edited small group curriculums and media for Sundays; led volunteer teams and Bible studies; helped with a regional women's event; and gave church announcements. In my thirties, I began teaching the Bible from the preschool classroom to the adults' midweek service—and anywhere in between. I started serving on the church's prayer team, speaking internationally, and writing books and Bible studies.

I've worked with various church denominations for more than fifteen years and am focusing my work this season on pneumatology (the study of Holy Spirit). God has been ministering the gift of prophetic encouragement through me for twenty years. I've had leadership oversight for over a decade as this gift operates within public ministry settings. I'm jumping into my forties, and I anticipate a variety of more adventures in store.

Most importantly, I have a husband, Matt, and two kids, Max and Zoey. Matt and I married in 2008 in California and later decided to raise our kids in northeast Florida. This was after a battle with the gloom and snow of upstate New York. My best friends and family are scattered nationwide, but we stay connected thanks to technology and weekly phone hangs. My greatest prayer is to see my family, friends, and self each grow into all God has for us.

Why am I telling you all this? Because I hope it stirs your thought process. You have been in training within your respective relationships and places too. From diaper changes to studying doctrine, it's all training ground for God. Even if you've been a Christian for one second, you gain guidance and assurance through the indwelling Holy Spirit; your training has begun!

More training happens as you study your Bible, gather monthly with a mentor, and serve at your local Bible-teaching church. It's one of the reasons I love the church—it's the greatest champion of God's people! One of my first mentors after becoming a devoted follower of Christ was my prom date's mom. She was a Catholic charismatic who loved Jesus deeply. We'd talk for hours about the things of God. The first-tier essentials unify us no matter our specific denominational beliefs or theological leanings within Christianity.

> From diaper changes to studying doctrine, it's all training ground for God.

To sum it up: I'm a mutt of Christian denominations and received ministry training through a hybrid of church environments. However, I will not budge from the first-tier doctrine beliefs and will always proclaim the power of our miraculous God! Now, what about you?

Pause and Reflect

1. Using the chart below, list how you've been in discipleship training and have undergone spiritual formation.

Training Ground	Past Training	Present Training
Places of Worship		
Biblical Education		

Training Ground	Past Training	Present Training
Serving at Church and Volunteering in the Community		
Relational Influences		
Other		

2. What are your denominational or theological leanings within Christianity?

3. What is your or your church's doctrinal view (system of beliefs) surrounding Holy Spirit? If you're unsure, check out your church's website for a better understanding of their beliefs.

It's Time to Go

As a woman of faith, a family member, a friend, and a leader in the community, you are a minister of the gospel. Whether or not you're in vocational ministry, you are called to play a part! Ministry is not only for those who get a paycheck; it is for all Christ followers. You minister in everyday life as

Theological Term

Spiritual Gifts—Holy Spirit ministers gifts powerfully through believers for the edification and equipping of the church. The manifestations of the Spirit are words of wisdom, knowledge, prophecy, faith, gifts of healing, working of miracles, distinguishing between spirits, speaking in various kinds of tongues, and interpretation of tongues. These gifts are based on 1 Corinthians 12:7–11. Alternatively called "supernatural gifts," "gifts of the Spirit," or "charisma."

you model God's love to your children when they refuse to do their homework, when you served your bestie her favorite meal after she lost her job, or when you pray for your coworker who is stuck in worry.

I can't help but wonder if God has placed you in some hard, out-of-your-control spaces because you know a miracle-working God. Hard spaces are not God's *discipline*; they are our spiritual *deployment*. Those in the military know soldiers are only deployed in strategic areas with tension. A soldier's presence keeps the peace. Similarly, what if God wants you to embrace where you are? What if you saw yourself as strategically positioned to fight the spiritual battles God has called you to? Fueled by God's Spirit, you are bringing kingdom-minded peace into your areas of position.

Remember, throughout the battles and beauty of this bumpy life journey, you've been trained and are ready. Just as my friend Ashley and I hid in the bathroom because of a spiritual struggle on the other side of that door, I knew this was when my training wheels came off.

> Ministry is not only for those who get a paycheck; it is for all Christ followers.

So, back to this ministry trip I started telling you about. As we prayed over a woman named Barb, the Lord ministered a word of knowledge through me. It was as if I knew this random fact about this stranger, so I asked, "Do you have nightmares that have been tormenting you?"

"How do you know? I haven't slept well in years and am constantly battling fear from trauma in the past."

God knew, and He wanted to set her free. After an hour of prayer and talking with Barb about faith, we knew God wanted to bring a deeper level of healing. Ashley gave her some ideas to journal through prayerfully, and we planned on meeting that evening.

It was as if we saw someone's house on fire, and she was crying out for help. We couldn't stand by and let it burn. We had the equipping of God's Spirit and understood that according to the biblical grid deliverance is for today, we had the tools to put the fire out, and we had fire insurance after calling my pastor. He reminded us we were covered and protected. Confident in God and armored with the truth, what followed that evening was remarkable.

Our new friend wanted freedom and heard from Holy Spirit in specific areas to pray and let go of. We partnered alongside her in agreement, declaring words of promise over her life. God doused some metaphorical holy water on that hellish fire and delivered her from the wreckage. This was my first time praying with someone to be free in this way, and God's Spirit empowered our prayer time for hours.

The specifics of Barb's story are not mine to tell, but I can tell you as we joined in prayer, a physical change happened. Something lifted off her. Her once rigid response was renewed as she confirmed a wave of peace washed over her. She left the event a completely different person, and you could even see a change in her eyes. Demons fled, demeanors changed, freedom was secured, and Jesus was glorified. Later at the event, every woman expressed they could feel the glorious Presence of God in that room. Barb has since reported back the nightmares stopped that day.

I can't unsee what I saw. Now realizing how much I've drastically ignored God's power in the past, I left refocused and determined to carry this momentum into my everyday life. It's time to run. God has given us free will to partner with Him in the mission of the kingdom. It's time to steward the ground God gave us and take back territory for the good. It's not us Christians against the world. It's us *in* the world. As we learn how to discern what's of God, find comfort from the Spirit, and embrace Him ministering through us, the reign of God's kingdom is prevalent. We aren't created to live passive, powerless lives. Just as God woke me up with those words that morning, I pray He uses them to encourage you too.

"You've been tiptoeing, but I've set your feet to run. You've been in training; it's time to go. There's a grid for this. There's a grid for this. There's a grid for this."

Spotlight of the Week

Figure 8. Promise-Keeping God
Two promises that bookend the narrative in Luke

Promise of Jesus	Promise of Holy Spirit
Zechariah was filled with the Holy Spirit (Luke 1:67) and began to prophetically declare redemption. He said that salvation "shows the mercy **promised** to our fathers" (v. 72).	Jesus told His disciples to proclaim forgiveness of sins. He then said, "Behold, I am sending the **promise** of my Father upon you. But stay in the city until you are clothed with power from on high" (Luke 24:49).
Zechariah was recounting the covenant promises in the Old Testament. The promised mercy was found in Jesus.	Jesus was recounting how He fulfilled the Old Testament covenant. He told His followers they would be clothed with power on high.

What does this mean for us?
Receiving God's promise of salvation through Christ alone fulfills the promise of His Spirit! Holy Spirit is God's promised presence in this present reality, and He empowers Christ's followers to endure in faith.

Day 1

PROMISES IN LUKE

What gift does Jesus promise to those who follow Him?

"While staying with them he [Jesus] ordered them [disciples] not to depart from Jerusalem, but to wait for the promise of the Father, which, he said, "you heard from me; for John baptized with water, but you will be baptized with the Holy Spirit not many days from now."

Acts 1:4–5

Pray

Holy Spirit, open my mind to understand Scripture to its fullest intent. Amen.

Read and Study Luke 24:45-53

I wish God promised us an easy life where we could healthily live on ice cream for every meal and have a daily family beach outing while frolicking with dolphins. That's the kind of pinky promise I can get behind. Unfortunately, the easy life is nowhere to be found in Scripture, so here I sit navigating some challenging situations, writing from a place of urgent desperation. Now, let me reassure you I'm not ministering from a place of doubt or discouragement

> **Context Is Key**
>
> The last act of Jesus' earthly ministry after the resurrection is what some call "The Great Commission" (found in Matthew 28:16-20, Mark 16:15-18, John 20:19-23, and Luke 24:45-49). Today, we are studying Luke's gospel account, which he also shared in Acts 1:1-11.

within these pages. But desperation to see a supernatural God invade my world that feels … well, *natural.*

I've already told you about my cyst scare that God resolved. However, that was just the start of this medical show. It feels as if I'm starring in my own medical drama, except there's no script, the plot keeps getting more convoluted, and the only autographs I'm signing are on my medical bills. An MRI of the brain, EKG of the heart, ultrasounds of various body parts, biopsies from my bone marrow to thyroid, and hundreds of blood tests have revealed more question marks than answers.

I'm sick of feeling sick. How about you? Is anything bringing weariness in your world? We must remember in the face of trials that God is not a thief, murderer, or destroyer—He is a promise-keeping, life-giving restorer.

God never promised us a perfect life on this side of eternity. He did, however, promise us Himself. The Christian faith poses a peace offering in the hard places. If life were painless, we'd stop looking for the Promised One who carries peace. Within that perspective we're enabled to run, walk, or sometimes crawl with God on this rarely straightforward, squiggly-lined path of life. Hey, any movement with God is a move in the right direction!

> God never promised us a perfect life on this side of eternity. He did, however, promise us Himself.

Here's a quick overview of the gospel of Luke. It is biographical in nature as it recounts the events of Jesus' birth and childhood (1:5–2:52), His preparation for ministry (3:1–4:13), public ministry and teaching (4:14–21:38), and conflict moving through the passion of Jesus (22:1–24:53). And get this: the words "promise" are bookends to the book of Luke (see figure 8, "Promise-Keeping God," on page 78).

After His resurrection, Jesus appeared and taught for over a month. In today's scripture, Jesus led His disciples out of Jerusalem but then asked them to return there. This was His final teaching moment. I wonder if Jesus led them out to instruct them to go back to Jerusalem because it presented a new opportunity: If He wasn't there physically, would they still physically follow Him? This was a chance for His followers to display their trust in Him as they were waiting and wondering. While waiting for the gift of God's Spirit, they remained active in the faith in three ways.

Christ's followers waited well by:

1. Worshipping together (Luke 24:52)
2. Obeying God's Word by doing what Jesus had asked (Luke 24:52)
3. Continually going to church and honoring God (Luke 24:53)

Here's some good news: we aren't waiting for God's Spirit like the disciples were post-resurrection. We *are* waiting for Jesus' return in the second coming (Acts 1:11). In our waiting for Him, we're also waiting to experience full redemption within a broken world. We're in waiting—for healing, for a relationship reconciled, for unity in the church. As we wait well, consider what Jesus told His followers, "I am with you always, to the end of the age" (Matt. 28:20).

We may be waiting to see Jesus face to face, but the promised power has already been poured out. He is with us until the end of the age. Holy Spirit is the promised presence that empowers us to wait well and trust God.

In the waiting, we live in active obedience with God. God is with us; we must remain in Him. Take any problems and praises and lay them at the Lord's feet. The question marks, the what-ifs, the worship, and the things entangled in your soul bringing doubt … lay them before God. *Wait.* Attend your local church. *Wait.* Make your kids their favorite chicken nuggets.

Wait. Study God's Word. *Wait.* Confide in your best friend. *Wait.* Pray for miracles. *Wait.* You get the idea. God promised us Himself—and that promise is fulfilled. Even while we are waiting, He is with us.

> Holy Spirit is the promised presence that empowers us to wait well and trust God. In the waiting, we live in active obedience with God.

Question

Review the three ways the disciples waited well. Is there anything different you need to be doing to wait well?

Day 2

PERMANENT RESIDENT

How do I know if God's Spirit is with me?

"Do you want to hand the keys of your soul over to the Holy Spirit and say, 'Lord, from now on I don't even have a key to my own house. I come and go as Thou tellest me'?"[2]

A. W. Tozer, *How to Be Filled with the Holy Spirit*

Pray

Holy Spirit, thank You for Your constant companionship. Amen.

Read and Study Luke 22:39–46 and Acts 4:23–31

On a particularly lazy Thursday around four o'clock, the doorbell startles me. I open the door and come face to face with a gentleman, probably in his sixties. He announces himself as the pest control guy. *Honestly, I wonder if he's a murderer.*

"I need to come in and check for water damage or anything that could indicate termites," House Guest says.

> **Context Is Key**
>
> Pre-resurrection and pre-Pentecost: Before facing betrayal, in Luke 22:39–46, Jesus went to the Garden of Gethsemane with His disciples. The same account in Matthew 26:36–46 shares that Jesus instructed Peter, James, and John to pray, and they fell asleep multiple times.
>
> Post-resurrection and post-Pentecost: In Acts 4:23–31, John and Peter gathered with other believers and prayed.

"Okay. But my house is messy."

With a chuckle, he quickly brushes off my worry about the messy state of the house. He carries a confident demeanor, assuring me lightheartedly he's got it all under control. A sense of ease and friendliness in his smile instantly puts me at ease too. It's as if he's saying, "No worries, I've seen it all!" His kind response makes me find comfort in my own house and reassures me he can handle whatever may be found.

As House Guest walks around, he never once comments on what I felt so eager to lead the conversation with. With care-filled attention, he examines every nook and cranny. He lights up the darkest corners with a flashlight, illuminating hidden spaces that rarely see the light of day. He's on a mission to uncover potential signs of trouble to ensure this house is secure from pesky intruders and filled with peace.

As House Guest ends the inspection, he shows me our coverage. "Your house has the best plan. If any invasion comes in, I'll take care of everything. We do damage control on anything and fix it all. That's with no extra charge. It's all been paid for."

As he circles the name of our plan, my author-mind is battling the desire to ask to borrow his pen. This is a sermon illustration in the making. *The price has already been paid for my mess.* I'm sure you see where this is headed …

Father God sent Jesus to fulfill a rescue plan through His death, resurrection, and ascension. The way John the Baptist shared Jesus to the world shows how Jesus would continue to carry out the rescue plan, as "the one who baptizes with the Holy Spirit and fire" (Luke 3:16; Acts 1:4–5). "Jesus' entire messianic mission consists in pouring out the Holy Spirit upon the world … one of the ways in which the risen Jesus continues His essential work, which is to baptize all of humankind 'in the Spirit.'"[3]

As you've welcomed Christ in, Holy Spirit dwells within. (I'll share more on this in week 3.) Holy Spirit is your permanent house guest and is of the utmost importance (Rom. 8:9–11). When your identity is rooted in Christ, Holy Spirit plays a crucial role in shaping, transforming, and empowering that identity; this is the evidence of His Spirit within. You are a disciple who lives for Him daily. Holy Spirit makes Christ followers the temple presence of God Himself (1 Cor. 3:16). Being a Christian isn't a onetime thing; it's your identity.

Will you let God's Spirit have full control, shining His flashlight in the dark cracks and crevices of your soul? This can be a complex and ongoing process as God does damage control, bringing about a metamorphosis in your life. He's doing a full remodel, which includes a whole new foundation. As He cleans out the cobwebs of addictions, gossip, or heartache, He replaces the emptiness with more of Himself. He isn't a visitor, He's a permanent resident and knows you better than you know yourself.

This is the God we worship, the One who frees us from ourselves, sin, confusion, and the corruption of rebellion. Give Him space to make Himself at home. God's rule is sovereign, good, and powerful. Even in a life filled with question marks, we can hand God the keys; He has a proven track record and is trustworthy. Holy Spirit guides and empowers believers and His church, helping its members to live in alignment with their Christ-centered identity. The Spirit convicts us of sin, leading to repentance and a desire for righteousness. He also enables us to display manifestations of His Spirit to benefit the church and the world.

> Being a Christian isn't a onetime thing; it's your identity.

As we welcome God's presence, our temple is under inspection and transformed into a residence of security and beauty. God fuels us with sustenance, advocates for us, and is gracious and kind. He even gives us good gifts to unwrap and use. Ultimately, Holy Spirit deepens our understanding of our identity, empowers us to live that out, and provides ongoing guidance, comfort, and transformation as we navigate our lives. We know God's Spirit is with us when we're with Christ. Give Him the house key and ask Holy Spirit to fill you daily. This is how we reside with Him!

Questions

1. What happened during the disciples' prayer time in Luke 22:39–46? What happened during the disciples' prayer time in Acts 4:23–31?

2. What are the differences in the disciples' behavior in the two passages? The disciples knew Jesus in both situations, so who can we attribute the change to?

3. What happened as they prayed and praised God (Acts 4:31)?

4. In your life, what dark places of pain or hurt is God shining His light in?

5. Since God is your house guest, how can you welcome Him to bring transformation? Why not do that right now through prayer?

Day 3

CLASH OF KINGDOMS

How does God stabilize me during spiritual warfare?

"The two lives engendered by the Spirit—the natural and the supernatural—are therefore never to be separated one from the other, and still less opposed to one another, but neither must they be confounded and put on the same level."[4]

Raniero Cantalamessa, *Come, Creator Spirit*

Pray

Holy Spirit, give me greater discernment and godlike mindfulness. Amen.

Read and Study Luke 4:1–13

There's a world we cannot see—a world with radio sound waves, Wi-Fi signals, and a spiritual realm where angels and demons are at war. There's a supernatural, spiritual battle all around us that impacts the human soul (heart, mind, and will) and the physical world. The visible and invisible worlds always intersect, whether we even realize it or not! Understanding the interaction of the two worlds is imperative in living Spirit-led.

Context Is Key

The story in Luke 4:1–13 occurs after Jesus' baptism when Holy Spirit descended on Him and before the start of His earthly ministry. Jesus was led into the wilderness by Holy Spirit. One theologian commented, "This is the first round of many battles Jesus will have with Satan and other demonic forces throughout Luke's Gospel. Though at points, like the crucifixion, it looks as if Satan wins, Luke tells us not to be fooled about who is the stronger force."[5]

This is for all those visual learners out there—cue God's organizational chart (see figure 9, "The Clash of Kingdoms," below). Every great business has an org chart showing the departments, ranks of positions, jobs, and functions. The spiritual kingdom is no different. Review the following chart (or download and print from jennyrandle.com/presence) to reference and better understand the cosmic battle.

Figure 9. The Clash of Kingdoms
The structure of God's org chart and what the supernatural battle looks like in the natural world

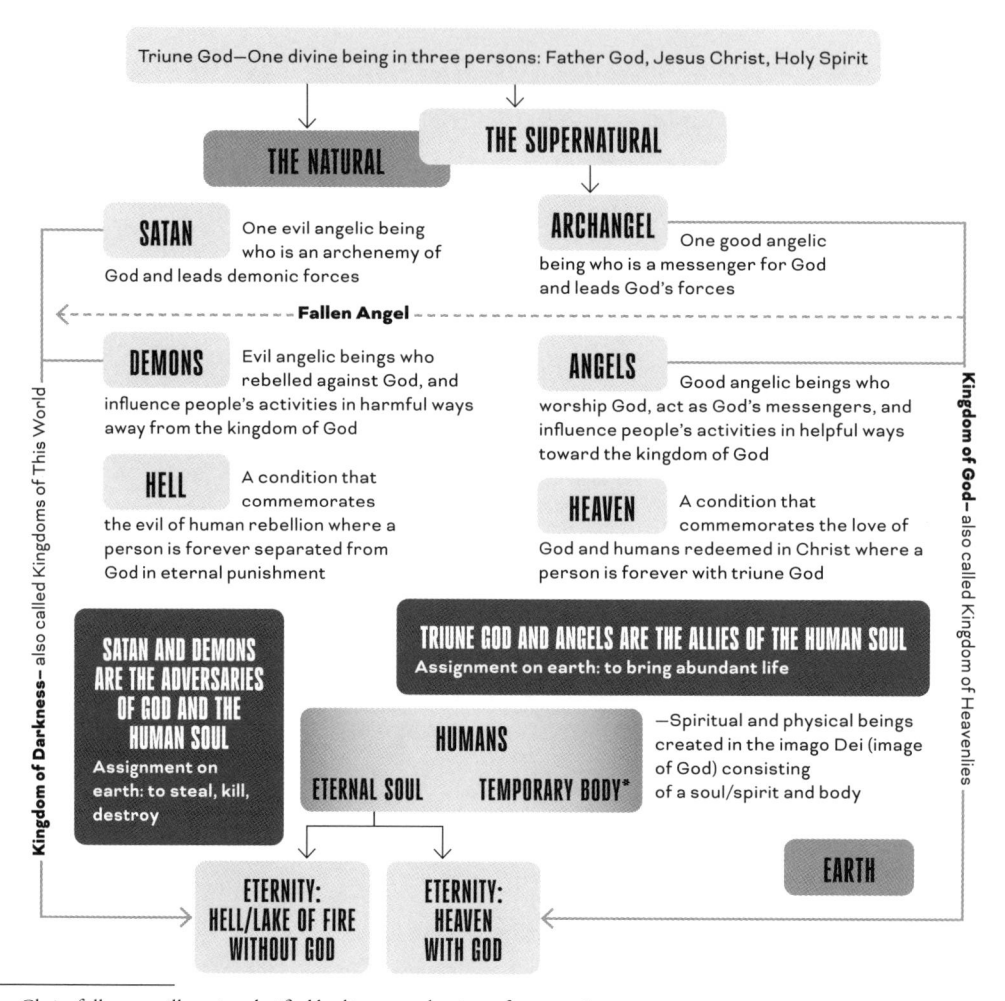

Triune God—One divine being in three persons: Father God, Jesus Christ, Holy Spirit

THE NATURAL | **THE SUPERNATURAL**

SATAN — One evil angelic being who is an archenemy of God and leads demonic forces

ARCHANGEL — One good angelic being who is a messenger for God and leads God's forces

- - - Fallen Angel - - -

DEMONS — Evil angelic beings who rebelled against God, and influence people's activities in harmful ways away from the kingdom of God

ANGELS — Good angelic beings who worship God, act as God's messengers, and influence people's activities in helpful ways toward the kingdom of God

HELL — A condition that commemorates the evil of human rebellion where a person is forever separated from God in eternal punishment

HEAVEN — A condition that commemorates the love of God and humans redeemed in Christ where a person is forever with triune God

SATAN AND DEMONS ARE THE ADVERSARIES OF GOD AND THE HUMAN SOUL
Assignment on earth: to steal, kill, destroy

TRIUNE GOD AND ANGELS ARE THE ALLIES OF THE HUMAN SOUL
Assignment on earth: to bring abundant life

HUMANS — ETERNAL SOUL | TEMPORARY BODY* —Spiritual and physical beings created in the imago Dei (image of God) consisting of a soul/spirit and body

EARTH

ETERNITY: HELL/LAKE OF FIRE WITHOUT GOD | **ETERNITY: HEAVEN WITH GOD**

Kingdom of Darkness— also called Kingdoms of This World

Kingdom of God— also called Kingdom of Heavenlies

---

*   Christ followers will receive glorified bodies upon the time of resurrection.

God's org chart would have two main structures under His rule: the supernatural and the natural. The spiritual realm (supernatural) is interwoven with the material world (natural). God made the cosmos, material world, and the spiritual realm. His power is by the Creator of power, Himself. He is all-powerful, all-knowing, and everywhere. The triune God (Father, Son, Holy Spirit) is sovereign, which means He has supreme control and reigns and rules over everyone and everything (Col. 1:16). King Jesus has all authority over the spiritual realm and the natural world. He will reign fully (Rom. 16:20), has reigned (Col. 2:13–15), and is reigning (Acts 26:18).

> **Theological Term**
>
> **Spiritual Warfare**—The ongoing battle between good and evil in the spiritual realm. Equipped with Holy Spirit, the believer's quest is to resist the kingdom of darkness and to remain close to God as they endure in faith.

Yet within these two realms are two competing departments: the kingdom of God and the kingdom of darkness. The leader of God's forces in the kingdom of God is the Archangel. The Archangel was created by God, and the other names are Michael, or the chief angel. Angels are also working in the kingdom of God. They are created by God, and their other names or types are ministering spirits, hosts, holy ones, cherubim, seraphim, and Gabriel (other than Michael, the only angel named). The Archangel's and angels' powers are mighty. Their function on earth is to free people from the control of sin and bring abundant life to humanity through connection with God.

The leader of the other "department" is Satan. God created Satan as a guardian cherub, but he ended up being a fallen angel that went rogue and created the kingdom of darkness. Satan's other names are Prince of Darkness, Prince of Demons, Devil, the enemy, Lucifer, ancient serpent, Father of Lies, the deceiver of the whole world, god of this world, and a tempter. God created demons as angels, but they, too, rebelled. Their other names or types are evil spirits, deceitful spirits, fallen angels, legions, god, unclean spirit, satanic powers, and principalities/rulers or authorities. Their function on earth is to produce evil in the world and lead people into rebellion against the will of God. Their power is limited, restricted, and confined.

God created humans who live in the natural world while encountering the supernatural. They have an eternal soul that dwells in a temporary body. Christ followers will receive glorified bodies upon the time of resurrection. God has given humanity free rein to partner with the kingdom of God or the kingdom of darkness. Of course, God wants us to partner with Him, but He doesn't force us. We are not puppets; we are people with the radical responsibility that comes from having our own agency. And God honors our choice. If one partners with God by believing Christ is their Lord and Savior, His Spirit transforms His people to share His moral character and empowers them to fulfill His purpose. The same is true if we partner with the kingdom of darkness. *Weighty, huh?*

As we've studied, Jesus did not fall into the temptation of sin (Heb. 4:15). The kingdom of God reigned regardless of the temptation from the enemy. This is the position Jesus' earthly ministry started: a posture of great obedience and security. Fueled by Holy Spirit and God's Word, the battle was won. Jesus did not fall for the enemy's temptation, although His earthly ancestor, Adam, did.† *If the enemy can't defeat God, perhaps he can defeat God's people.*

In everyday living, you are purposed to enjoy God, bring Him glory, and make a good and godly impact on others. However, an enemy seeks to derail these efforts as He looks for ways to prevent God's plan. It's important to remember battles do not disqualify us from our purpose. Part of that entails recognizing we have battles to fight! **During spiritual warfare, Holy Spirit brings discernment and wisdom while acting as our rudder, guiding us closer to God and helping us stay on course. He is our stabilizer, steering us toward a steadfast faith.**

What do we categorize as spiritual warfare? Anything that robs us of God's abundant life (John 10:10). Here's the deal: we will never respond perfectly to the enemy's schemes and will never be void of sin on this side of eternity. You are not Jesus. This temptation narrative we have studied today isn't about you; it shows the deity of Christ incarnate (in human form). Praise God, there is a God who was and is sinless and perfect! Father God sent Jesus to defeat the Devil and bring freedom to those who place their trust in Jesus through salvation. We need Him.

God's people are empowered with Holy Spirit to confidently abide in God, resist the evil one, and strengthen the church. As you face temptation and tricks against the enemy, remember sin has no control over you; arm yourself with Scripture and be filled with God's Spirit.

---

† Study the genealogy of Jesus (Luke 3:23–38) to see Jesus' blood relatives from Mary's line.

> Holy Spirit is our stabilizer, steering us toward a steadfast faith.

Questions

1. Reviewing figure 9, "The Clash of Kingdoms," what are some key takeaways you want to remember?

2. In Luke 4:1–13, how did the Devil tempt Jesus?

3. What two weapons did Jesus use in His battle against the enemy? How is knowing that helpful for you?

4. As you live for God, in what specific ways are you aware of the enemy working against you?

5. Holy Spirit is a rudder guiding you to stay on course with God. If you were to write up battle plans to fight any temptation or heartache you or a family member is facing, what would the plan look like? How does knowing that God is there to help and guide you influence the plan?

Day 4

DECEPTIONS FROM CONNECTION

What holds me back from knowing Holy Spirit?

"God withholds Himself from no one who perseveres."[6]
St. Teresa of Ávila, *The Life of St. Teresa of Jesus*

Pray

Holy Spirit, draw me closer to You. Amen.

Read and Study Luke 11:9–13

Have you ever been sitting next to someone and still not been paying attention to them? Just yesterday, my husband was talking about the yard makeover, and I didn't hear his question about the mulch because I was scrolling on my phone looking at teal bread makers I would probably never use. We're in a world of distraction, and it is costing us something: connection. We are missing connection with

> **Context Is Key**
>
> Luke 11:9–13 takes place during the earthly ministry of Jesus right after He taught His disciples how to pray. This was pre-Pentecost and shares God's desire for them to receive His Spirit.

one another and God Himself. This lesson shares four major deceptions around our connection with God. It's time to stop being distracted and dive in!

Four deceptions harming our connection with Holy Spirit:

1. Manipulative lies
2. Misrepresentation of Holy Spirit
3. Misunderstanding who Holy Spirit is
4. Missing or dismissing the Spirit altogether

Manipulative Lies

Last week, my dog peed on the couch in my favorite sitting spot. I know, gross! I went to tell her that was wrong, and she dramatically looked away. I moved her closer to my face. She looked the other way. This repeated multiple times. Her guilt led her to avoid making eye contact. Her feelings of shame led to trouble responding to acts of intimacy. Feels familiar, huh?

One of the greatest lies is feeling as if we can't approach God. I wonder if shame is the main thing holding us hostage from being vulnerable before a very forgiving, loving, and available God. We feel unworthy, flawed, tainted, inadequate, or even humiliated, so we don't run to the thing we should. We look away.

But God.

Work through the lies harming your God-given identity. God is setting apart His followers (sanctification). God has made you whole in Him, purified by His Spirit, and capable and empowered to live on a mission for Him and because of Him. Look at Him! Shame lifts, and the lies flee when a woman turns from sin, learns her worth in God, and stays close to Him.

Misrepresentation of Holy Spirit

The unfortunate reality is that Holy Spirit has been used as a manipulation tool.[*] Some individuals and groups have twisted a move of God, or spoken a word, for personal gain or to push

---

[*] The last three deceptions are more public displays of faith. There can be extreme expressions on both ends of the spectrum. Some may not intentionally try to deceive others, and others may have an evil agenda altogether. God gives us discernment.

their own agenda. Some have even begun to chase the gifts of God more than God Himself. I have had spiritual leaders physically shove me down in a prayer line claiming supernatural healing when the only healing needed was their ego.

Christians misrepresenting Holy Spirit have caused skepticism and caution among many. Instances where believers have acted inappropriately or claimed actions in the name of Holy Spirit while contradicting His character can create roadblocks we must navigate. These experiences can seep into our souls and make us cynics. Guard against that. Contending for a genuine move of God is one of the greatest prayers we and our local churches should be praying. Being on the receiving end of healing as a woman prayed for me has been instrumental in my own life. If I had been closed off toward God's ability to minister through others, I wonder if I would have missed out?

> Contending for a genuine move of God is one of the greatest prayers we and our local churches should be praying.

If we remain humble, love people, prayerfully consider our hearts' agenda, and are motivated to serve God and God alone, we can represent God properly. Holy Spirit can also help us discern the deception in those who can't. Remember, displaying godly character and God's power should be synonymous.

Misunderstanding Who Holy Spirit Is

Misunderstanding Holy Spirit can cause confusion and misinterpretation of His role and presence in our lives. Remember, the Bible is our grid, and our pneumatology fits within biblical boundaries. **If the Spirit of God is at work, the experience will align with the Word of God and His character.** When these are aligned, we're correctly interpreting

Holy Spirit. If anything is outside of the grid, use caution. God's Spirit will always point people to Jesus.

Although a move of the Spirit isn't always *normal*, normalizing a Spirit-led life should be. When one lacks an understanding of Holy Spirit, it hinders them from fully embracing God's transformative work and the Spirit ministering through their life with gifts of prophecy, faith, and healing, for example.

Contending for a supernatural move of God while sustaining theological integrity can feel convoluted, but it is a worthy cause. Walk in the Spirit while maintaining boundaries within the grid. Attending a local church that believes in supernatural gifts and teaches from the biblical text on a Sunday will also strengthen your understanding of the Spirit.

Missing or Dismissing the Spirit Altogether

The last deception harming your connection with Holy Spirit is ignoring Him altogether. He is a person of the Trinity—worthy to get to know. If you neglect to know who Holy Spirit is, you're neglecting God Himself.

Some think God is not actively ministering supernatural gifts to strengthen the church. This theology can lead to a more limited understanding of God's sovereignty and goodness. Or diminish the expectation of divine intervention and downplay the significance of spiritual gifts in contemporary Christian practice.

A leader approached me because she was going through some trials. She felt comfortable asking our ministry for prayer, so she vulnerably shared what was happening. The Ministry of Desperation was not foreign to her. I knew she usually held the cessationist view, but sometimes, desperation invites us to do some new things.

> **Theological Terms**
>
> **Cessationism**—Extraordinary manifestations of God's presence and power, as shared in biblical accounts, are restricted to a specific time and are no longer accessible or relevant to believers today. Those who hold this doctrine believe gifts like healing, distinguishing spirits, and speaking in tongues ceased in the apostolic age.
>
> **Continuationism**—God is continuously involved in the lives of believers with the potential for ongoing miraculous experiences. Those who hold this doctrine believe the gifts of the Spirit continue and are for today.

Before our meeting, I walked Ally through how our prayer gatherings go and mentioned our prayer team is open to the Spirit ministering through our time together. I showed her in Scripture how this could be through the gifts of prophecy, words of knowledge, or any other biblical way the Lord deemed fit. She agreed to meet, and we prayed together days later.

During that time, the Spirit ministered detailed and specific words no one knew about Ally's situation. We gently guided her through this half an hour of prayer filled with encouragement over her family, her teaching gift, and the pain she was walking through. She confirmed that what our words and Scripture shared was of the Lord and brought great comfort. Ally left shocked that she was so known, valued, seen, and loved by Him. This moment deepened her relationship with Him as she encountered a very real and present God.

Addressing the areas challenging our connection with Holy Spirit is essential. Seek God's Spirit. Theological integrity and a belief in supernatural encounters can coexist within our lives and the lives of our churches. By being open to a move of God in healthy environments, we experience the fullness of His transformative power, strengthened community, and vibrant and contagious faith.

Questions

1. How does Luke 11:9–13 shape your thinking around the four misconceptions toward connection with God?

2. What harmful lies do you believe about yourself that don't align with who God says you are? How do these lies cause you to look away from God? Ask Holy Spirit to guide you toward the truth.

3. Describe a situation where someone misrepresented Holy Spirit. How has this made you cynical toward desiring things of the Spirit?

4. Would you consider yourself holding more of a continuationist or cessationist doctrine? Have these beliefs helped you or held you back from knowing God?

5. Reflect on a time someone represented Holy Spirit with a proper biblical understanding. How did that help your connection with God flourish?

Day 5

ACTS OF PROCLAMATION

Why is Holy Spirit with me?

"You will receive power when the Holy Spirit has come upon you, and you will be my witnesses in Jerusalem and in all Judea and Samaria, and to the end of the earth."

Acts 1:8

Pray

Holy Spirit, give me the boldness to share the hope of Christ with others. Amen.

Read and Study Acts 9:31

I invited my friend Rebecca to pray over my ministry team during an online work meeting. Rebecca volunteers in her church, has a history of demonstrating accurate prophetic words, and I trust her to minister with compassion. At this time, my ministry team was a handful of people spanning the United States, with one woman in South Africa. As Rebecca prayed over women she had never met, it was as if she were reading their mail. God's Spirit ministered through her by confirming callings, providing comfort in situations we had no knowledge of, and pointing them toward Jesus.

Rebecca's child, who was potty training at the time, came in and had to use the bathroom. She angled her phone away from us, lifted her child onto the toilet, and boldly continued to pray. On this day, Rebecca's acts of proclamation spoke words of comfort to sisters around the globe while meeting the needs of her toddler.

This reminds me of another friend who volunteered as a singer on her church's worship team. She'd place her one-year-old in one of those infant walkers during worship practice and protect his little ears with headphones. He did so many laps in that sanctuary as his mama sang songs of praise.

Perhaps proclaiming God's goodness requires a flexibility within our own agendas and schedules. I think of my husband who was out for a bike ride on the Newport Beach boardwalk and spotted a man who seemed to need shelter and warmth. Matt turned around and rode the three blocks home on this brisk fall night, grabbed his only jacket, and chased this man down. "God loves you, man!" Matt proclaimed as he gave him his winter coat. In all of these situations, we see being fueled by God's Spirit is living servant-hearted in both the unseen and seen missions God has placed before us.

This week, we learned how God's promised Spirit indwells the believer, what God's power looks like within the spiritual battle around us, and what can hold us back from knowing God. We also learned who is with us while waiting for Christ's return (Holy Spirit), and today, we're learning why He is.

Holy Spirit empowers people to call on the name of the Lord for salvation (Titus 3:5–6), for deliverance from the consequences of sin and death, and for making disciples. In the book of Acts, we see proclamation and kingdom-powered action. The message of faith in Christ is to be proclaimed to all the nations.[7] We can miss out on this mission when we play it safe or are too busy doing all the other things.

God doesn't want us in a "safe" religion. Safety is not even a fruit of the Spirit. Safety is not a spiritual gift. Safety was never a promise of God's kingdom. But security is. As a Christ follower, you are secure in Him and sealed by God's Spirit. As we read in Acts 9:31, Peter walked in fear of the Lord and found comfort in Holy Spirit, and the church grew. This is a model for us. Comfort from Holy Spirit and the safety of religion are two drastically different things. In fearing God while being comforted by His Spirit, the kingdom reigns on earth as God manifests His presence amongst us and within us.

Luke wrote the book of Acts differently than he wrote his gospel. He wasn't tracing a person's life; he was tracing places. Acts tells of the acts of Holy Spirit as the gospel is proclaimed geographically. Jesus' words in Acts 1:8 anchor the main components of the book. Once the Promised Presence fell on the day of Pentecost, *all* of Jesus' disciples in Jerusalem were filled with God's Spirit (2:4). The gospel went forth and the message of Christ was proclaimed through Jerusalem (2:14–7:60), Judea (8:1–3), Samaria (8:4–40), and to the ends of the earth (9:1–28:31). Christ followers are living out the metaphorical Acts 29, sharing the same proclamation.

The kingdom of God and His Spirit are interwoven. His kingdom cannot be established without His empowerment. "Biblical Witnesses on Mission" (figure 10) is not exhaustive but highlights the beginning of the early church. Review the scriptures on the next page. The early church grew as Christ followers boldly shared the truth. Miracles followed proclamation, with the most significant miracle being salvation!

> The kingdom of God and His Spirit are interwoven. His kingdom cannot be established without His empowerment.

Figure 10. Biblical Witnesses on Mission

Examples of the early church expanding as Christ is proclaimed

Witness ⟶	Mission ⟶	Miracles
Early church believers	Acts 2:42	Acts 2:43 Acts 2:47
Peter and John	Acts 3:6 Acts 3:15–16	Acts 3:10 Acts 3:21
Apostles	Acts 5:12	Acts 5:14–16
Philip	Acts 8:5	Acts 8:6–7
	Acts 8:12	Acts 8:12–13

Two things brought about the church's growth: a move of Holy Spirit and persecution. Studying the theology of Holy Spirit within Acts, we see Holy Spirit empowering Christ followers to be witnesses for Christ, and both Jews and non-Jews testify to the truth of who He is. As God's mission goes forth, the primary purpose of God's Spirit is revealed. He's bringing about transformation, deepening one's relationship with God, and empowering effective service in fulfilling His will.

The second way the early church grew was through persecution. Life is hardly free from danger, especially the Christian life (especially for the early church). In Acts 1:8 and 22:20, the noun for "witness" in the original Greek language (*martus*) goes beyond *just* sharing the truth of Christ. "Witness" refers to an individual or group that may have been killed due to sharing their testimony (a martyr). We see this through the martyrdoms of Stephen (7:54–60) and James (12:2–3) and the persecution and suffering of other apostles like Peter (vv. 3–4) and Paul (21:31–32). Five thousand people came to faith after the arrest of Peter and John (4:4).

Our witness is directly connected to our relationship with God. Our proclamation is found in receiving His power (Holy Spirit)! The supernatural kingdom of God is where we must live within the natural world, even within our own suffering and that of others. We must stop looking away from the toxic, tainted, and troubled things around us because we

WEEK 2—THE PRESENT REALITY OF GOD'S SPIRIT

don't want to rock the boat or those in it. **Holy Spirit is with us to help us proclaim the gospel as we press on and enjoy God until everything is fully redeemed.** There is more to life than addiction ravaging your family line, hate tearing apart a Bible-teaching church, and secret sin holding you hostage. Share God's truth, proclaim His promises, and pray down heaven!

Holy Spirit equips you to show up and stop being distracted or hiding from present-day pain. And remember, you aren't anyone's Savior; you're pointing people toward the One who is. A woman who knows how to speak boldly is a woman bent toward heaven. We're ready to walk on purpose and proclaim the hope of Christ because we know we've been given God's power to do just that! These lessons are a call to embrace a deeper relationship with the present reality of a God who loves you deeply.

> A woman who knows how to speak boldly is a woman bent toward heaven.

Questions

The book of Acts mentions *Holy Spirit* more than any other book in the Bible. As we live mission-minded, remember God's Spirit is the One doing the ministry! Look up key attributes of Holy Spirit and how He impacts us. Note them on the lines below:

Holy Spirit, like Jesus, is a covenant _____ from Father God (Acts 1:4; 2:33, 39) and a source of _____ (Acts 1:8; 4:33; 6:8; 10:38).

To Christ followers, Holy Spirit is also _____ (John 14:26), _____ (Acts 11:12), and will _____ you (Luke 12:12).

In Acts 4:8, the apostle Peter was _____ with Holy Spirit, and in verse 13 people saw _____ on him.

People shared _____ about the kingdom of God (Acts 9:27; 14:3; 18:26; 19:8; 26:26; 28:31).

Holy Spirit helps you in your _____. "For we do not know what to pray for as we ought, but the Spirit himself _____ for us" (Rom. 8:26).*

BENEDICTION

"By his divine power, God has given us everything we need for living a godly life. We have received all of this by coming to know him, the one who called us to himself by means of his marvelous glory and excellence. And because of his glory and excellence, he has given us great and precious promises. These are the promises that enable you to share his divine nature and escape the world's corruption caused by human desires" (2 Pet. 1:3–4 NLT).

---

* Answers: promise, power, a comforter, guide, teach, filled, boldness, boldly, weakness, intercedes.

WEEK 3 PRE-SESSION QUESTIONS AND TEACHING VIDEO

Community Connection

Start off the discussion by sharing some "Yay God" praiseworthy moments from the week. Taking time to celebrate how you see God moving is pivotal in recognizing a God on the move.

Learning Theology

- This past week, we read about the present reality of God's Spirit. Our "Spotlight" was on God's promises, and how when we receive God's promise of salvation through Christ, it fulfills the promise of His Spirit! What stood out to you in this week's lesson regarding Holy Spirit?
- See page 74, question 1. From diaper changes to studying doctrine, it's all a training ground for God. In reflecting on your discipleship training and theological leanings, how have your theological views about God's Spirit been impacted?

- See page 98, question 4. Would you consider yourself holding a continuationist or cessationist doctrine? Has practicing this doctrine helped you or held you back from knowing God?

Watch Jenny's Lesson 3 Teaching: Holy Spirit and God's People

URL: davidccook.org/access

Code: Presence

Living Out Theology

- As Jenny mentioned, from creation to the completed story, Holy Spirit's activity has been an empowering agent for God's people. Share a time you've felt the empowering presence of God.
- What spiritual practice do you find the most helpful in receiving Holy Spirit's companionship?
- This week's reading focuses on a question found in Acts 19:2: "Did you receive the Holy Spirit when you believed?" How do you think you'd explain this concept to a child?

Prayer Team

There's power in prayer! Give everyone a piece of paper or use the Prayer Cards downloaded at jennyrandle.com/presence. Who do you know that needs to know Jesus? Write down a prayer request asking God's Spirit to awaken that person to a saving relationship with Christ. When finished, fold the paper for the group leader to randomly distribute the Prayer Cards. Pray over the request you received this week. If you're able, send the person you're praying for some encouragement!

This Week

Read week 3 and answer the corresponding questions.

Week 3

THE FELLOWSHIP OF GOD'S SPIRIT

"Did you receive the Holy Spirit when you believed?"

Acts 19:2

After graduating in 2004 from a private college in New York, I vowed to never go back to school. God had other plans, though. In the fall of 2022, I enrolled in seminary, working toward a master's at Asbury Theological Seminary. Having an undergrad degree in television/radio, I took core classes consisting of analyzing TV shows and producing videos. This grad work in academia was a whole new world of reading hundreds of pages weekly while taking a full class load and juggling family responsibilities and ministry work. Talk about a plot twist!

A few weeks into my second semester, I did some back-to-school decluttering to get my head in the game. I tackled the daunting task of purging files off my computer and found a flyer I designed in 2007. It was for a church event we were hosting, and the bold orange text caught me off guard: "If you can't see God, maybe it's time to look a little closer."

I began to wonder: Was I viewing God only through the lens of my pain, or was I looking for Him to infiltrate every facet of my life? Did I need to look closer? My theology knows He's a God who can be trusted, but do my actions live out that reality as I juggle the day-to-day tasks and trials afforded to me? I know God, but am I intimate with Him in all areas?

This book was never meant to delve into the depths of my brokenness or mess. Initially, I intended to craft a narrative solely around the immense power of God, accompanied by bold and sweeping statements about how the church as a whole may be inadvertently manipulating or misunderstanding the work of Holy Spirit. While I still hold conviction in those assertions, I recognize the heart of the matter is less public and way more personal than I initially planned. That totally sounds like God, doesn't it? He moves us from general theories to intimacy with Him. I'm learning to search for God in both the pain and purpose. Holy Spirit is present in all the areas I welcome Him to and is constantly pointing me to Christ.

Posture of Desperation

During the start of this second semester in seminary, I saw God in a way I never had. After what seemed like a standard chapel service for a Christian university in Kentucky, the students quickly learned that day was far from ordinary. On Wednesday, February 8, 2023, three students at Asbury University stayed after chapel to pray together. This sparked an outpouring of God that led to genuine repentance, praise, prayer, and healing for students around the world.[1]

Although living in Florida, I attend the seminary across the street for my grad work, taking online classes with the option of attending onsite as needed. Even the online students at Asbury Theological Seminary started to hear rumblings about what was happening at the university.

By Saturday, the internet was abuzz with what was happening on campus. People were sharing clips online, national news outlets were reporting about this genuine move of God, and there were testimonies of lives being transformed. Oh, how I wished I could be there. God's Spirit filled the students up as the theology of the head collided with the heart. There were no bells and whistles. No famous speaker or celebrity worship leader. People had an authentic hunger to see God, and He met them there with a powerful outpouring of His presence.

I continued to be intrigued by the work the Lord was doing at Asbury. Days after the outpouring of God began at the campus, on Monday, February 13, I got an email from one of my professors, Thomas McCall. It was titled "A Brief Update: The Surprising Work of God" and confirmed what we'd been hearing. Below is a paraphrased version of what he shared:

> The presence of God was so real. No one wanted to leave. Word spread and people started running, literally running to the chapel. By that evening, the chapel was full. They sang together, read scripture, and prayed together. Some students prayed all through the night. The next day students poured in and stayed all day Wednesday, Thursday, and Friday morning. Friday evening. And Saturday morning, the chapel was overflowing with people ... This chapel service has been going continuously for over 100 hours ... It is just so obvious there is a hunger and thirst for righteousness ... People are in the presence of something astounding and have this deep sense of joy and peace that is overwhelming ... This is a foretaste, a glimpse of heaven. When you taste it, we realize this is what we are made for, and we don't want anything less ... No one planned this. No one orchestrated this. No one is controlling this. We don't know what the Lord has for us, but we are really, really grateful.[2]

The same day, a friend who was also watching what was happening texted, "Are you going to take a trip to Kentucky?" It was the push this nonspontaneous gal needed. Two days later, around 10:00 a.m., I was headed to the airport.

Let me tell you—God is in the details. While boarding my first leg from Florida, my friend Kimberly texted me about Asbury. By the second leg of my flight when I checked in with her, her tickets were purchased for the next day. I'm thankful we roomed together, stood in long lines with frozen toes, and shared protein bars for most meals. Her coming sorted out details I didn't even think to plan out properly. Plus, Kimberly is a singer-songwriter, so worshipping God next to her sounded beautifully angelic. It was a gift to experience these modern-day miracles beside a friend in the faith.

What God birthed from a few students' desperation grew into an outpouring of His glory. You can't manufacture or manipulate a move of God like this. There was no performance. You cannot sustain days of continuous worship without the empowering of Holy Spirit. He was healing His people. This posture of desperation and crying out from the younger generation was answered by a loving God.

It was a place where heaven invaded earth, and our only response was to worship in awe of triune God. I saw the older generation praying over the younger, the younger leading the older, interdenominational unity, and the sweetest sense of God's presence. Everything was stripped away except the tangible evidence God was with us.

Approaching God

As Kimberly and I worshipped at Asbury from the front row of the balcony, we had a view directly over the worship team on the stage. We could see the altar was a flurry of activity, although you wouldn't know it if you were sitting on the floor level. The time at the altar was a private affair. I was moved by what I could see happening. A grown man weeping as students gathered around praying, a young woman knelt at the altar as someone simply sat with her flipping through pages of the Bible, and mixed ages and ethnicities danced and worshipped together in the aisle.

Before I knew it, I felt prompted by Holy Spirit to walk down two flights of stairs and into the auditorium's main floor. I approached an older woman whom I had never met before but had been watching from the balcony. I could tell she was a firecracker in the faith; she carried a spunky passion in her worship, drawing me in. I watched her pray for others and felt led to ask her for prayer too. After introducing myself, I asked her to anoint me with oil as I was battling chronic illness. She prayed. She reminded me of the grandmas of faith at the church where I became a devoted Christ follower. She declared healing, spoke peace, and many other things I can't remember. Her love for Jesus was evident, and even though this was our first meeting, her compassion and love were obvious.

I don't know what happened during that prayer other than one thing: I felt God weigh me down like a weighted blanket. So, we sat together on the worn floor that had been walked on by countless college students and leaders. It was a fresh filling of the Spirit, and I can promise you this: I left different than when I arrived.

A Glimpse of Heaven

Kimberly and I left the building, and what we thought had been two hours actually had been seven. We had worshipped God for seven hours and could have stayed longer. There was no sense of time as we gathered corporately, worshipped, prayed, repented, and celebrated all God was doing. By the time we left days later, multiple locations were hosting overflow sites, and I was told the line of people waiting to get in was over half a mile long. Yet still, there was so much more to behold. This outpouring of God's glory at Asbury lasted more than 380 hours. Sixteen straight days of encountering the glory of God; I can only imagine this is what heaven will be like.

I've been to a wide variety of "religious" events in the past, like tent meetings, planned revivals, miracle nights, and liturgical services practicing the sacraments. What happened at Asbury was not planned, nor would I categorize this as any of those events. I've studied historical movements within Christianity like Phoebe Palmer's impact on the Holiness Movement in 1840 and Duquesne University's impact on the Catholic Charismatic Renewal in 1967. In both, there was interdenominational unity, testimony, prayer, and a desire for God's Spirit. The Asbury Outpouring of 2023 was like that. Prayer was met with a spontaneous move of God, which created a revival-like atmosphere resulting in the pursuit of holiness and receiving Holy Spirit.

How God showed up to minister to His people was not an over-the-top, out-of-control expression of the gifts. It was sacred ground, and God empowered the leaders to steward it honorably filled with joy, love, and compassion. This was heaven invading earth as God breathed life into His people.

God poured out His Spirit at Asbury. In that sanctuary, the reverence and awe toward God was something I'd never witnessed before corporately. I've felt it in my private prayer time with God, but together with thousands of others worshipping the true God—the experience was so sacred and sweet I could barely talk about it. I didn't want one word spoken back to me that held ill intent or doubted God's work. Yet I share this with you to preserve the sacredness of what I witnessed, and I pray the same outpouring extends to our families, churches, and the world!

God with You

We don't always get to hop on a plane to see what God is doing. Nor do I think we should. We may not fully understand it in our finite brains, but an infinite, powerful God meets His people with His glory. And here's the beautiful thing—His glorious Presence is not just contained in the walls and halls of Asbury. We don't have to chase revivals, outpourings, or awakenings (call it what you want) to experience a move from God. The same God who filled that space is within you. Through a relationship with Jesus, this same sustaining power is for you too. Our greatest response to a move of God should be one of awe and deep gratitude that a God who loves us this much would fellowship with His people.

God restores the broken and lost and revives us to life, and often, these moments catalyze in prayer. I've been mulling over what it means to be a carrier of prayers that wear the potential of such promises. To think: the Spirit of God Himself is within. The same God who was at Asbury is the same God who can meet you at your local church, during your daily activities, or in your secret place of prayer.

Fellowshipping with God is what being a Spirit-filled Christian is! This week, I'll expand on the key differences between indwelling, baptism, and filling of the Spirit.

Pause and Reflect

We see throughout Luke and Acts how God was not only preparing people to go to the ends of the earth with His truth, but He was powering them up to do so. Being a follower of Christ encompasses the belief in and adherence to the teachings of Jesus, the recognition and response to the triune God, and the participation in bringing heaven to earth through the work of Holy Spirit. We have this one wild life we've been entrusted with as we live for Jesus.

Review the following chart (figure 11) for a summary of the ways Holy Spirit is close to His people. How have you experienced Holy Spirit fellowshipping with you?

Spotlight of the Week

Figure 11. Holy Spirit's Fellowship with Followers of Christ
Showing the relationship between God's Spirit and His people and how He interacts in three ways

What	Indwelling of Holy Spirit	Baptism of Holy Spirit	Filling of Holy Spirit
	Companion in the Christian life	*Companion with Power*	*Companion Post Conversion*
	Your life becomes a marker for the presence of God.	Your life becomes fully immersed in the power and presence of God.	Your life becomes a powerful mission with the presence of God.
Spirit Perspective	Guide believer's life with the lens of the Spirit	Empower believer with the power of the Spirit	Minister through believer with the power of the Spirit
Your Perspective	Transformed life	Powerful life	Mission-minded life
What Do You Do?	Receive Jesus	Participate	Participate
When Does This Happen?	Salvation/Conversion	Unclear when in Scripture, but this is when the believer encounters God's Spirit in power	When believer cooperates with God
How Often	Once (permanently) at conversion/salvation and indwells the believer continually throughout their Christian life	One time as an event either at salvation or separate occurrence	Continually throughout the Christian life
Power Grid	Romans 8:9 John 14:15–17 Ephesians 1:13–14 1 Corinthians 6:19	Luke 3:16 Acts 2 Acts 8:14–17 Acts 11:16	Luke 4:1 Act 4:31 Acts 11:24 Acts 13:52

The Spirit is both a gift and a person to participate with. Spend time with your ever-present House Guest and be filled to overflowing. We're embracing Jesus is alive and actively transforming lives, building the church, and creating disciples. As the Spirit is at work, families are changed, communities are set ablaze, and you're living out the will of God.

Day 1

INDWELLED BY LOVE

What's the heart of the matter?

"I trust that this sweet fire of the Holy Spirit will work in your heart and soul as it did in those holy disciples."[3]

Saint Catherine of Siena, a letter to Pope Urban VI

Pray

Holy Spirit, dwell within me and empower my heartbeat to be in sync with Yours. Amen.

Read and Study Acts 15:6–12

"God loves me." This was the phrase I urged women to repeat when I was on a panel at the 2024 est.HER Conference outside of Nashville. As the room full of women echoed the phrase, Holy Spirit quickened my spirit and gave me a word of knowledge. I didn't declare a "Thus says the Lord," but simply said from the stage, "Even when I asked you to say 'God loves me' out loud, I got the sense someone said *no* internally and literally

Context Is Key

Our following passage takes place during Paul's ministry journeys, a time when the gospel was expanding beyond the Jewish community. In Acts 15, the Judean believers were teaching that in order for Gentile believers to be saved, they needed to be circumcised, according to Jewish law and customs. Paul, Barnabas, and others were sent to the Jerusalem Council to discuss if the Gentile converts had to uphold this law. This passage shares a pivotal point in church history as the council determined what faith in Christ looked like and who salvation was for.

can't say those words ... If that's you, we'd love to pray for you at the close of our time." As we wrapped an hour later, a woman responded.

Holy Spirit brought her discernment in knowing the word of knowledge was for her. She told me that as the ladies surrounding her declared God's love, she said out loud, "Nope, can't do it. I can't say those words." I hugged her tight as we prayed in the sanctuary. This beautiful woman knew the love of Christ in her head, but it had a hard time penetrating her heart.

Later in the weekend, the prayer team also prayed with her as we trusted the Lord to further strengthen her identity in Him. You know what the key to her freedom was? As we were praying, someone urged her to begin praying out loud different character traits of God, whatever Holy Spirit brought to her mind. It wasn't because God forgot who He was; it was to remind her own spirit and to speak truth over her broken heart. "God is kind. God is compassionate. God is just ..." and she ended proclaiming "... and God loves me!"

> **Theological Term**
>
> **Indwelling of Holy Spirit**—The permanent residence of God within a person who professes faith in Jesus Christ as their Lord and Savior, establishing a personal and transformative relationship.

This reminds me of the apostle Paul's view on religion. He felt that "religion without God's power transforming the heart was useless."[4] God's Spirit reminds us that as daughters of God, we don't need to silence any shortcomings; we show up with God's perspective, trusting He has made us holy and continues to make us holy as our hearts are positioned toward His. In welcoming Christ in and handing the keys of your house over, Holy Spirit envelops you with His love. We're already cleansed, clean, purified. We're new. Our transformation is pivotal!

The Old Testament echoes the promise God will rescue and restore His people. In Deuteronomy 28–30, Moses brought a proper warning of rebuke toward the Israelites and the judgment that would follow from their disobedience. If the Israelites broke the covenant, curses would follow. Moses also gave an invitation to repent so they might receive a blessing through their faithfulness to God. In Deuteronomy 30:6, Moses declared, "The LORD your

God will circumcise your heart and the heart of your offspring so that you will love the LORD your God with all your heart ..."

Let's pause on that word "circumcise." I know this is a bit of a leap from chatting about period cramps or menopause with the gals, but let's lean in for a minute. In a male-dominated tribal culture, marking the male reproductive organ through this ritual was a form of tribal identity. The Egyptians also circumcised as a rite of passage to mark purity and fertility. Clearly, circumcision language was familiar to the ancient Near East. Circumcision was a sign within the Abrahamic Covenant (Gen. 17). For Israel to walk in the covenantal blessing, Moses was saying, metaphorically, that their heart must undergo the same process to cultivate a purified, genuine, and undivided love toward the Lord.

> We don't need to silence any shortcomings; we show up with God's perspective, trusting He has made us holy and continues to make us holy as our hearts are positioned toward His.

The recorded words of the prophets assure us God transforms hearts to enable covenant-keeping people—like a promise within a promise. First, God will put His Spirit within His chosen people (Ezek. 36:27; 37:14). Second, exchanging the heart of stone for a new heart is undergirded by a promise of an everlasting covenant (Jer. 32:40). This covenant foretells a promise for God's Spirit to reside within His people. It declares freedom for the exiled (Jer. 31:34).

These historical principles are echoed before the religious leaders in the passage we are studying today. In Acts 15:6–12, after much debate, Peter addressed the Jerusalem Council by emphasizing that God has also given His Spirit to the Gentiles, which shows no distinction between them and the Jews. As Paul explained how Jesus cleansed the Gentiles' hearts through faith, he reinforced the concept of a metaphorical circumcision, highlighting that true purification and inclusion into God's covenant comes from an inner transformation rather than external traditions.

This circumcised heart—rather than a circumcised body—becomes a marker of spiritual purification, demolishing barriers separating one from God. **God's Spirit is doing heart surgery, regenerating, and resuscitating hearts to beat in sync with His.** As the story unfolds, the everlasting covenant mentioned is found in Jesus—the new covenant. This circumcised heart is a marker of the Christian identity. The promise of heart transformation through God's Spirit is pivotal to restoration. The new covenant promises the Spirit doesn't just come upon God's people but within them. This is one feature that makes the new covenant new and complete.

Yes, we must remember even in this natural world, even when the glass may seem full, it is still cracked. The water is tainted with poison leaking from the broken glass, making a mess. Someone needs to clean this up. This is where a broken-glass world meets the Creator of the world. Christ has rescued us from the poison and positions us with purpose and a heavenly perspective. The Father sent the Son, and those who know Christ intimately are indwelled by God's Spirit within.

Salvation equips us to show up for God because we've been free from sin and death and transformed to walk with Him. Through faith in Christ, the power of the Spirit renews our inner being, transforms our hearts, and reminds us of our identity. We are women of freedom within a world being redeemed. God indwells you, and His love is for you too.

> We are women of freedom within a world being redeemed. God indwells you, and His love is for you too.

Question

"God loves me." Say that out loud. Are you able to embrace that truth? Acts 15 is a passage that affirms Gentiles can be followers of Christ along with the Jews. In verses 7–8, how do you see the cleansing of hearts connected to the fellowship of God's Spirit?

Day 2

BAPTIZED WITH GOD'S PROMISE

Why is Pentecost important today?

"I [Peter] remembered the word of the Lord, how he said, 'John baptized with water, but you will be baptized with the Holy Spirit.' If then God gave the same gift to them as he gave to us when we believed in the Lord Jesus Christ, who was I that I could stand in God's way?"

Acts 11:16–17

Pray

Holy Spirit, guide me toward a biblical perspective of Pentecost. Amen.

Read and Study Acts 2:17–41

When we lived in New York, our nondenominational church included Pentecost on the church calendar. It was a service where we learned about the first time God's Spirit

> **Theological Term**
>
> **Baptism with Holy Spirit**—A one-time defining moment in which the empowering presence of Holy Spirit becomes a tangible reality, actively immersing and shaping one's life. This moment is often equated to when the believer receives the Spirit and responds to His power, enabling one to walk in obedience to Christ.

was poured out to Christ followers. Those Sundays were a beautiful remembrance and invitation to receive whatever the Spirit wanted to impart.

Pentecost was the day the promise in Acts 1:4–5 was fulfilled as God poured out His Spirit to empower His people to go to the ends of the earth as His witnesses (Acts 1:8). As the promised Spirit came from heaven sounding like a mighty rushing wind, He filled the entire place where the disciples of Jesus were. Divided tongues of fire appeared and rested on each one. They were all filled with Holy Spirit and began to speak in other tongues as the Spirit gave them the ability to speak out. The crowd gathered and was bewildered their native tongues were being spoken. The different groups of people heard the disciples declaring the mighty works of God. Some were amazed, and others began to mock them, saying they were drunk. Peter addressed their concerns, recounted Joel's prophecy, and preached to the crowd (Acts 2:2–41).

They encountered the power of God during this Pentecost event. The baptism with the Spirit is a single moment that provides a perspective shift for the believer. God is tangibly felt for the first time after Jesus departed. Pentecost was a moment when the supernatural power of God came upon all the believers in that place and empowered them.

The Spirit baptism didn't stop with the Jewish Christians. In looking at the different accounts in Acts, we see two types of evidence from receiving God's Spirit. First, there is an endurance to share the gospel and walk in obedience to God. Second, there are immediate manifestations of God's Spirit in the individual's life.

Figure 12. Receiving Holy Spirit and Church Growth
Four biblical accounts of how, when, and the result of Spirit baptism

Acts 2 | Jewish-Christian

Believers gathered at Pentecost ⟶ Holy Spirit fell (vv. 1–4) ⟶ Holy Spirit ministered with tongues and rested on them (v. 3) ⟶ Amazement (v. 7) ⟶ Peter's first sermon (vv. 14–40) ⟶ 3,000 added to the faith (v. 41)

> **Acts 8:15-25 | Peter and John Prayed for New Believers in Samaria**
>
> New believers (v. 15) ⟶ Leaders prayed and placed hands on them (v. 17) ⟶ Received Holy Spirit (v. 17) ⟶ Continued preaching gospel to villages of Samaritans (v. 25)
>
> **Acts 10:34-48 | Gentile-Christian**
>
> Peter shared the gospel (vv. 34-43) ⟶ Holy Spirit fell on new believers (vv. 44-45) ⟶ Holy Spirit ministered through them with tongues and extolling God (v. 46) ⟶ Amazement (v. 45)
>
> Note: Pivotal moment in Christian history shows the Christian faith is for both Jew and Gentile, which widens the growth of the church.
>
> **Acts 19:1-10 | Disciples in Ephesus**
>
> Paul asked John the Baptist's disciples if they had received the Spirit (v. 2) ⟶ Responded no (v. 2) ⟶ Shared full gospel of Christ (vv. 4-5) ⟶ Laid hands on them (v. 6) ⟶ Holy Spirit came upon them ⟶ Holy Spirit ministered through them with tongues and prophesy (v. 6) ⟶ Paul stayed for two years so *all* Asia residents heard word of the Lord (both Jews and Greeks) (v. 10)

I've heard this Pentecost event called a lot of different things: "receiving the Spirit," "baptism of the Holy Ghost," "Pentecostal outpouring," or to use Jesus' words, "baptized with the Spirit." Spirit baptism is crucial and contributes to our spiritual formation, devotion to God, and ministry. I believe baptism with the Spirit is a onetime event for the believer as they have a personal experience realizing the empowerment of God's Spirit. It is a moment marked by God's Spirit enabling the believer to walk out the fullness of the Christian life in obedience to Him.

I was baptized with God's Spirit when I was eighteen, just months after my conversion to Christianity. As I experienced God's power, the Spirit ministered through me, manifesting power through glossolalia (speaking in tongues). This gift became my greatest asset during prayer (1 Cor. 12:10, 28).

> Spirit baptism is crucial and contributes to our spiritual formation, devotion to God, and ministry.

Every major Christian tradition believes in the baptism of the Spirit, but with slight variations of interpretation or definition. Some say being filled with Holy Spirit is the same as the baptism of the Spirit. The Catholic interpretation of Spirit baptism is viewed as creating an awareness of the sacraments. The Reformed view the baptism of Holy Spirit as the indwelling of the Spirit at salvation. While the classical Pentecostal view holds the view that Spirit baptism happens within a second occurrence and that speaking in tongues *must* follow as initial evidence. Perhaps this is why many neglect the work of the Spirit, as the details can be considered controversial or confusing.

These differences are not first-tier doctrine issues, and they don't impact salvation. However, I am challenging us ladies to acknowledge the power of the Spirit and that godly fruit, and His gifts, are imperative in the life of every believer. Therefore, I separate the fellowship events from Holy Spirit because they are significant. God's Spirit indwells the believer at salvation; He baptizes with power and brings subsequent fillings enabling us to do our tasks in obedience to the will of God.

The promise of the outpouring of the Spirit is an invitation to be responded to, no matter one's leadership title, ethnicity, age, or status. The Spirit of God is for the equipping of His people. As we saw in figure 12, the Gentiles got saved by hearing Peter preach, God's Spirit was poured out, and they began speaking in tongues (Acts 10:34–48). For them, being baptized in the Spirit happened at salvation. Scripture shows it also occurs simultaneously when you get baptized by water (Luke 3:21–22), through the laying on of hands (Acts

19:6), during prayer (8:17), or within a separate occurrence (19:1–10). After receiving God's Spirit in power, people were amazed, the church grew, and the gospel went forth!

Pentecost is a critical event where God's presence dwelled with His people. Pentecost matters because it's when God's Spirit immersed Himself as the powerful and personal Presence of God in Christ followers' lives. This is a miracle, just as the birth of Jesus is.

> The promise of the outpouring of the Spirit is an invitation to be responded to, no matter one's leadership title, ethnicity, age, or status.

Being baptized in the Spirit means the believer's life becomes fully immersed in the power and presence of God—this is what true Christian living looks like! And the result is a church enduring until they are face to face with Christ! The baptism with Holy Spirit is a onetime event Christ followers should pursue (if they haven't) and reflect on (if they have). God is renewing His people with His presence and power to walk a life of obedience!

Questions

1. On the day of Pentecost in Acts 2:17–21, Peter gave his first sermon about the last days from Joel 2:28–32. In the following chart, look up the verses on the right and draw a line connecting them to the correct passage on the left.

Connect Acts 2:17–21 to Scripture	
Power Grid "In the last days …"	**Connect the Text**
Your daughters shall prophesy (Acts 2:17)	Acts 11:27–28
Your young men shall see visions (Acts 2:17)	Rom. 10:13
My male servants and female servants … and they shall prophesy (Acts 2:18)	Acts 21:9
I will show wonders in the heavens above and signs on the earth below (Acts 2:19)	Acts 16:9–10
The sun shall be turned to darkness and the moon to blood (Acts 2:20)	1 Thess. 5:2
The day of the Lord comes (Acts 2:20)	Matt. 24:29
Everyone who calls upon the name of the Lord shall be saved. (Acts 2:21)	Acts 5:12

2. Read Acts 2:36–41. What was Peter's invitation? What would the people receive if they accepted it?

3. What resulted from Pentecost after Peter gave his first sermon?

4. When was the first time you encountered God's power and presence?

5. What do you believe about the baptism with the Spirit after reviewing the biblical evidence?

Day 3

FILLED WITH GOD'S PRESENCE

How do post-conversion encounters equip me?

"The people of God, who walk according to the Spirit, live in bold contrast to flesh-walkers. Their minds are set on the things of the Spirit (their minds have been renewed by the Spirit, after all); in place of hostility to God, they live in peace; and instead of death, they know life."[5]

Gordon Fee, *Paul, the Spirit, and the People of God*

Pray

Holy Spirit, fill me with Your Presence. Amen.

Read and Study Acts 13:52

Remember how the Spirit is like an invited house guest? Well, the filling of the Spirit is the moment the guest takes over every room of the house. Except this is a good thing—not like the overstepping invasion the time Aunt Sally stayed over! Holy Spirit was already present, dwelling within, but

> **Theological Term**
> **Filling of Holy Spirit**—The continuous experience of surrendering to Holy Spirit's influence and empowerment, resulting in transformation and alignment with God's will in a believer's life.

now He extends His influence to every corner of the house overflowing into the neighborhood. Being filled with God's Spirit represents a deep sense of the Spirit's active and pervasive influence in every aspect of our lives. It's as if the house guest, who was once working behind the scenes, now takes center stage and transforms the atmosphere of the entire house with His vibrant presence and power, leaving tangible signs of Jesus that even pour into the community.

Holy Spirit empowers His people for assignments and provides supernatural revelation. God's Spirit fills His people with power and provides His perspective. Subsequent fillings of the Spirit occur throughout your Christian life after receiving Him, producing a boldness and endurance to be a witness for Christ and build the church (as seen in Acts 4:8; 13:9). As Holy Spirit fills you, your job is to be present and participate. You surrender, seek, and remain open to His empowering and guiding presence. You *get* to notice Him at work, respond in obedience, and submit to His leadership. As you do, He helps you pray, proclaims the Word, strengthens you to overcome spiritual opposition, produces godly fruit, convicts, sanctifies, guides, advocates, provides wisdom and power, and ministers with gifts.

I'm reminded of my friend Megan and how she prayed for years for more of God. While attending a typical church service, she told me, "This warm feeling washed over me during worship. I started crying and sweating, and it felt overpowering. I knew it was God. A veil of grief had been following me for a year after the death of my dad. The darkness was lifted off that day." As Megan cooperated with Holy Spirit, He moved *through* her with His power, resulting in an inward change and outward manifestations of His presence. As Megan felt the power of God, her depression lifted, and she was filled with more joy and peace. What I love most about her story is Megan confidently tells people about her fellowship with God's Spirit. Proclamation and healing go hand in hand!

We all have different situations affecting our assignments throughout life, yet there's a unity of purpose. We have one purpose and one corporate mission as a church. Our assignments are God-instructed, and our purpose is to bring God glory and enjoy Him within the callings and circumstances of life.

The Bible provides numerous examples of distinct callings and individuals being equipped for their missions. Mary, the mother of Jesus, was equipped to carry the Son of God (Luke

1:26–38). Anna, a prophetess in the temple, interceded, fasted, and proclaimed the message of Christ (2:36–38). Joanna and Susanna were empowered to support Jesus' ministry (8:1–3). Lydia, a wealthy business leader, was prepared to host church leaders (Acts 16:14–15). Tabitha was known for her good works and charity (9:36). Priscilla was tasked to assist Paul in ministry (Acts 18:1–3, 18–28; Rom. 16:3–5). Philip's daughters were gifted as prophets (Acts 21:8–9). These biblical women helped start and sustain the early church and shared the gospel. They received grace and were able to embody God's power through their talents and tasks. This is the same for you.

No matter the task or assignment, your tank is not empty; God is filling you for the mission. It's not *you* the world sees; it's *Jesus in you* that captivates the room. Don't shrink back, because it's time you show up. Maintain that Spirit-led perspective! You are not too loud, too quiet, overbearing, or underwhelming. God has commissioned and called you and will empower you to lead with compassion and strength. He has set you apart for this time in history. God is aiding you with His Spirit and filling you with His perspective to share the gospel and strengthen the church!

In depths of desperation, when all options seem exhausted, behold the power of God. He is the source of unwavering faith, joy in sorrow, and brings a peace that surpasses all understanding. When you lack confidence in ministering to your family, friends, or within the church, behold the power of God. God's powerful love is tangible, His fellowship is close, and He fills you to overflowing!

Questions

1. Acts 9:1–22 shares Paul's journey of conversion. What happened during Paul's baptism in verses 17–19?

2. What happened to Paul in Acts 13:9 so he could rebuke a false prophet?

3. Pick one of the following passages to read about Paul's ministry adventures: Acts 14:1–7, 8–18; 16:16–24; 16:25–40; 19:11–20; 20:9–12; 27:21–44; 28:3–6; or 28:7–10. How do you see Holy Spirit filling him in his ministry tasks?

4. Reflect on a time when you or someone you know was filled with God's Spirit and it directly impacted your family or church family.

5. How does understanding God's ability to fill you encourage your next steps?

Day 4

SANCTIFIED TO BE SET APART

How does developing godly fruit make a difference?

"What hope we have for when the whole world is finally fully filled with heaven again, but until then, we get to bring a piece of heaven to everyone we meet!"[6]

Jessie Fox, missionary in Argentina

Pray

Holy Spirit, I welcome You to continuously transform me into the likeness of Christ. Amen.

Read and Study Luke 16:10–12

Although this book mainly focuses on the ministering power and authority of Holy Spirit, it would be dismissive of me not to mention His power within. After all, we are women who demonstrate godly character and wield God's power. One who claims Christ as their own shouldn't be full of hate, in despair, impatient, agitated, mean, evil, faithless, harsh, or out of control. The sanctifier, God Himself, transforms you and empowers you to develop love, joy, peace, patience, kindness, goodness, faithfulness, gentleness, and self-control (Gal. 5:22–23).

Holy Spirit opens your eyes to Jesus in conversion and transforms you into an image bearer of Christ. God's Spirit applies your salvation as you become who you behold. This transformation is not just for your eternal glory but to bring God's glory to this side of eternity.

Within His residing presence you have been changed, are changing, and will continue to change as you look more and more like Christ. This process is called sanctification.

Jessie and Daniel Fox returned home to the States after helping build a ministry in Honduras. They are cross-cultural servants (missionaries) with Signs of Love, a ministry that seeks to bring sign language and the love of Jesus to the deaf in rural areas worldwide. When the COVID-19 pandemic paused their plans to establish in a new country, they ended up living stateside in our island community.

God led Jessie to the beach during a prayer event my ministry hosted. After an hour, I introduced myself and asked her if she needed prayer. With tears, she said, "You already prayed for me." It "just so happened" that on this day we had been praying over missionaries. I had no idea and was overwhelmed by a God who cares.

Jessie later told me God used this prayer event as a catalyst to help her begin to hear His voice again for the first time in over ten years. After the prayer time ended that day, God's Spirit ministered through Jessie to give a powerful and personal prophetic word to a stranger that was encouraging, comforting, and edifying.

As Jessie and her husband continued to meet new friends, they got involved with a local church. I noticed Jessie always made herself available. When I asked her if her strategy in serving God differed from overseas, she said, "I felt God instruct me to simply show up." So, she showed up. She ironed tablecloths for church gatherings, prayed at hospitals, dropped off flowers on doorsteps, invited new friends into her home, and baptized people. One woman went home to be with Jesus shortly after Jessie baptized her. Later, Jessie had the opportunity to baptize this woman's son while serving at a kids' summer event. I can only imagine this moment was an answer to a mother's heartfelt prayers, now echoing through eternity.

Each day Jessie tangibly demonstrates being the hands and feet of Jesus. She has this way of always loving locally by making herself available for the "small stuff." Yes, she held on to her "bigger" dreams for the future, but she never seemed to diminish the present place God had her positioned. She postured herself toward God with a heart to serve; fruit followed, and His love was evident to those around her. Through her, our local church was strengthened, and individuals deepened their relationship with God because of her service.

As Jessie offered herself by showing up, God surrounded her with discipleship opportunities and deep friendships. Two years later, these same friends were gathered on the same beach as that first prayer event that had started it all for Jessie. These friends prayed these servants off to their next ministry adventure to share the gospel in Argentina in rural deaf communities and beyond as they continue to show up for people.

When I texted Jessie the other day, she shared a few ministry updates with me. As we continued to talk, she reminded me of God's goodness, even in suffering, illness, and lack. Our relationship with the triune God brings us assurance. In the waiting, we can still find the sustaining and sanctifying work of His Spirit, and in the end, we will be fully restored.

God's sanctifying work also enables us to uphold a moral set of ethics, walk in His will, develop godly habits and character traits, and love Him and others. **As your faith is rooted in Christ, the fruit you yield empowers you to worship Him and model Him to others. It's a pruning process to grow good fruit as you walk with the Spirit.**

Sometimes we show up and our stinky attitude follows as we ignore, reject, or look right past people God has placed in front of us. Jealousy leads to gossip, comparison leads to insecurity, disregarding the needs of others magnifies our own selfishness, and bitterness entangles roots of resentment within us. Rotten fruit is gross for everyone who touches it.

But God.

In the growing pains of sanctification, we are comforted by a God who cares and loves us deeply. As we receive the ministry of God's Spirit, repentance follows closely. God removes ungodly traits and refines our mindsets and heart postures. He untangles the thorny vines of deception that spread fast and cause harm and confusion toward His truth. He uproots the weeds of sin that are stealing our light. He provides nutrients through His Word as the Spirit breathes life and growth into us. The pruning process is worth it, though; the fruit God's children yield is evidence of a loving God. Holy Spirit is a personal God who invites us to flourish, transforming us into Christ's likeness and enabling us to champion the church as we show up for others and shine bright for Him.

Questions

1. What is the key character trait of God highlighted in this lesson?

2. In Paul's writings to the Galatian church, he listed the fruit of the Spirit (Gal. 5:22–23). What fruit needs to ripen in your life? How are you going to be intentional about growing this trait?

3. As you prayerfully reflect on your personal life, within your local church family, or beyond, consider how Holy Spirit can minister within you or through you. What does this require of you?

4. In the parable in Luke 16, Jesus teaches the importance of using wealth wisely. In a broader view, it's about being faithful with the small stuff (v. 10). How does Jessie's story model that?

5. Is there anything God is asking you to be faithful in? What can you do to continue to walk out the Spirit's sanctifying process?

Day 5

TRANSFORMED TO BE FREE

What does biblical deliverance look like?

"Thou movest us to delight in praising Thee; for Thou hast formed us for Thyself, and our hearts are restless till they find rest in Thee."[7]

Saint Augustine of Hippo, *Confessions*

Pray

Holy Spirit, help me pray and walk into greater freedom. Amen.

Read and Study Luke 8:1–4

As I stepped through the double doors of the mental health facility, a chill ran down my spine. It was as if I had crossed a threshold into a world that no longer belonged to me. The cold, sterile waiting room echoed with distant whispers and hushed conversations while the flickering fluorescent lights cast an eerie glow on the worn linoleum floors. The air seemed heavy with despair, and the faint scent of hand sanitizer mingled with the murky aroma of forgotten dreams and mistaken identities.

> **Theological Term**
>
> **Deliverance**—Being saved and/or set free and liberated from captivity, harm, or the enemy's schemes demonizing or destroying your life. True deliverance is found in the God of the Bible.

I had stepped into a behavioral healthcare office, but it seemed more like a psych ward. My medical insurance had pointed me there, and I was grateful for the help, but I was unprepared for the other level of care that was being offered there. Some people paced back and forth, holding lengthy conversations with themselves, another helped their struggling child, and one woman sobbed, pleading for the proper paperwork to give to the judge so she could regain custody.

Within these walls, individuals battled their inner demons. Their haunted eyes reflected a deep sense of isolation, each one silently pleading for liberation from their own personal darkness. The hollowness in a person's eyes was not foreign to me. It was the same void and emptiness I often saw while ministering to those who needed freedom from harmful things. There was no light of Christ or glimmer of hope found.

Remember, there's a cosmic battle raging in the spiritual realm. Sometimes, you can physically see the battle. On this day, I did. This was a place teetering on the edge of restoration, where some souls struggled to find solace. Amongst the turmoil and strife, it seemed as if they were lost; image bearers of Christ clouded in a fog of forgotten identity (Gen. 1:26).

I, too, was there to face some storm clouds. Even though I'd been serving the Lord for more than half my life, I needed practical support for the anxiety that felt like a wet blanket over my daily activities. I'd done the spiritual work by seeking out freedom and deliverance, having friends pray over me in parking lots and on phone calls and asking advice from trusted advisers. **My hope in Christ moved me to get further help in my calamity.** After all, I knew God brings movement within the areas that often lay motionless.

"Jennifer."

No one responded. I looked around and then hesitantly stood. "Randle?" I said as I was ushered through the doors. In the sterile room, I was told to step on a scale. Then, the nurse handed me a cup of pills and instructed me to change into a gown. "I'll be right back with your shot."

Scenes from the iconic movie *One Flew Over the Cuckoo's Nest* flashed through my mind. I was shocked but not into silence. "This doesn't seem right," I told the nurse, who stared at me blankly.

"You're Jennifer, right?" She then proceeded to go through all of Jennifer's meds.

"Jennifer *Randle*," I stated firmly.

"Oh, my goodness. These are *not* for you." She grabbed the pills back as fast as her face fell. "This could have gone horribly wrong!" She quickly ushered me back into the waiting area. Sitting in silent wonder, I texted Matt the SOS emoji and did not move again until my full name was called around thirty minutes later.

We're in a daily power struggle. This power struggle can feel like a three-ring circus, juggling the trifecta of the mental, physical, and spiritual components of what makes us, *us*. I had been caught in a case of mistaken identity. Agreeing with that identity would have poisoned me. If I hadn't advocated for myself, I would have partnered with the wrong things.

Holy Spirit is our advocate and guide, helping us fight the enemy. God has given us three tactics we can use. First, we are to put on the whole armor of God and stand against the Devil's schemes (Eph. 6:10–18). The Bible instructs us to give no space to the Devil (4:27) and to be intentional about resisting him (James 4:7).

Second, God not only equips us but empowers us through His Spirit. He has given His disciples authority over the enemy (Luke 10:19). God in you is greater than he (Satan) that is in the world (1 John 4:4).

Third, do not be overcome by evil, but overcome evil with good (Rom. 12:21). The good is God. Goodness is produced from living a life for God and with Him. We are to love Him with all our heart, soul, and mind (Matt. 22:37). Goodness always follows.

> **Theological Terms**
>
> **Stronghold**—A place, thing, or being that has a hold over you. Often connected to spiritual warfare, strongholds are barriers and obstacles between someone and God that hold a person back from true freedom and victory. However, strongholds are not always negative. The Lord can be your stronghold too (Ps. 9:9; 18:2).
>
> **Biblical Freedom**—Liberation is found in Christ. The New Testament strongly asserts humans cannot overcome the grip of sin in their own strength. This truth finds confirmation in the realities of our modern world. Despite our sincere intentions to do what is right, evil often proves too formidable for us. We cannot accomplish the good deeds we aspire to (Rom. 7:21–23). Thanks to Christ's redemptive work, sin's power has been shattered. Through the law of the Spirit of life in Christ Jesus, we have been liberated from the law of sin and death (Rom. 8:2).[8] Freedom is beyond a moral compass; it's a lifestyle.

You are called "Christ follower," and you are to follow Him. Your identity in Christ finds freedom in Him. As we follow Him, we're women who break generations of unhealthy patterns, and sin isn't controlling our actions. This is deliverance. As we walk in the will of God, we find freedom from addictions as God's Spirit manifests self-control. Torment, strongholds, lies, isolation, gossip, sexual immorality, greed, bitterness—the list could go on and on—are rendered powerless. We may not always respond perfectly to the power struggle, but we will not be poisoned. We find freedom as Christ's love is found.

This lesson barely scratches the surface of the complexities of being delivered and set free. Continue to study this in Scripture! Freedom is a byproduct of being a child of God. The work of Holy Spirit within God's children is evident by godly transformation, freedom, and receiving and demonstrating His power as the Spirit ministers through your life.

> **The work of Holy Spirit within God's children is evident by godly transformation, freedom, and receiving and demonstrating His power as the Spirit ministers through your life.**

Just as it is with healing, freedom from something (in my case, anxiety) can come in an instant, a process, or within eternity. I am set free, and being set free, in a world that is broken! I do know this, though: we can't expect full union and fellowship with the triune God when we neglect Holy Spirit. Who are you approaching when your world feels toxic or shattered? If you haven't had the onetime experience where the power of God became real to you, pray for the baptism with Holy Spirit, and receive Him. Do you seek a filling of the Spirit? Be intentional. After being in a refining fire with the Spirit, you will not leave the same way you walked in. God can be trusted. Go to Him. May we approach Him, not just for answers or calm, but for intimacy and closeness. As we've learned, Holy Spirit fellowships with us by indwelling within, immersing Himself with us (baptism with the Spirit), and filling us to overflowing with His power and presence.

Questions

1. Grab your Bible and look up some freedom encounters. In Luke 8:1–4, who was healed and what were they healed from?

2. In Acts 8:6–8, how did the demonized manifest? What was the result?

3. How did Paul get rid of the evil spirit in Acts 16:18? Write out the exact words.

4. As the disciples ministered in Acts 19:12, what left the people?

5. What has a stronghold on you? Do you need freedom from anything? Prayerfully consider what deliverance looks like for you. Process through any lies or poison from the enemy, and exchange them for the truth of God's Word. What can you do this week to empower yourself or others into God's freedom?

BENEDICTION

"Peter said to them, 'Repent and be baptized every one of you in the name of Jesus Christ for the forgiveness of your sins, and you will receive the gift of the Holy Spirit'" (Acts 2:38).

WEEK 4 PRE-SESSION QUESTIONS AND TEACHING VIDEO

Community Connection

Start the discussion by sharing some "Yay God" praiseworthy moments from the week. Taking time to celebrate how you see God moving is pivotal in recognizing God on the move.

Learning Theology

- This past week, we read about the fellowship of God's Spirit. Our "Spotlight" was on how Holy Spirit indwells, baptizes, and fills His followers (see figure 11, "Holy Spirit's Fellowship with Followers of Christ"). What stood out to you in last week's lesson regarding Holy Spirit?
- Every major Christian tradition believes in the baptism of the Spirit. How has this been taught to you? Reread the definition on page 121. What are your thoughts on this viewpoint?

- See the questions on page 139. After looking at some of the freedom encounters, how does Holy Spirit equip Christ followers for the work of deliverance? How does your local church help people find greater freedom?

Watch Jenny's Lesson 4 Teaching: Private Spaces and Public Places

URL: davidccook.org/access

Code: Presence

Living Out Theology

- As Jenny mentioned, our private moments with God shape and mold us for our public platforms. What else did you take away from her teaching?
- How do you see Holy Spirit empowering courage within someone in your church community?
- This week's reading focuses on Jesus' words in Luke 8:46: "Someone touched me, for I perceive that power has gone out from me." When have you encountered God ministering powerfully to you or a family member? How did you participate in that moment?

Prayer Team

Do you need a fresh filling of God's Spirit? Are you in need of transformation in a certain area? What has a stronghold on you? There's power in prayer! Write down a prayer request focused on how God's Spirit wants to fellowship with you or your local church (filling, transforming, healing, bringing freedom, or developing godly character). Then fold the paper and the group leader will randomly pass out the Prayer Cards. Pray over the request you received this week. If you're able, send the person you're praying for some encouragement!

This Week

Read week 4 and answer the corresponding questions. As we wrap up, don't miss the Common Questions material in week 5. Write down any insights and ideas that come from that reading to discuss at your final group meeting.

Week 4

THE POWERFUL WORK OF GOD'S SPIRIT

"Jesus said, 'Someone touched me, for I perceive that power has gone out from me.'"
Luke 8:46

"While the Spirit is everywhere, He is not everywhere in the same way," Dr. Bounds stated. This led to a conversation with my seminary classmates about the omnipresence of God and our desire to have Him be present in a palpable way we can comprehend. As we pray the plea, "Holy Spirit, fill the Church, fill me and my household," we're asking a supernatural God to be naturally present in a discernible way. The class ended with my professor saying, "We're operating in the fumes of something that took place one to two hundred years ago. We need a fresh movement of God's Spirit."

Father Raniero Cantalamessa, a Catholic priest and scholar, has described God's power and fire as a red-hot iron. He's shared that, historically in the medical field for wounded or diseased parts of the body, the treatment plan consisted of fire. Surgery was nearly all cauterizing with a red-hot iron. Fire was a remedy for the sick and hurting. But healing by the fire doesn't come to those who talk about it, listen to others talk about it, or even watch others get burned.

The fire transforms the one who touches it.[1] We aren't the fire starters. We're the burned and diseased needing to be touched by the fire of God. The fresh movement of God's Spirit comes as He wills and when His power touches His people.

Since 2014, my journals have been filled with petitionary prayers seeking revival and miracles. I knew if people felt God's power, they'd leave on fire for Him. Since then, I've learned that God's powerful work is beyond comprehension. Even attempting to expand on the scope of God's power feels convoluted. However, in starting the conversation, I hope God uses it to light a spark in your soul. This conversation is not comprehensive, and like most things with the triune God, there is depth beyond what we see on the surface.

> The fresh movement of God's Spirit comes as He wills and when His power touches His people.

So far, you've read how Holy Spirit is God's present reality in this present day. In week 1, we studied miracles and what to do in the unraveling of challenging circumstances. Empowered by Holy Spirit, both Jesus' earthly ministry and the early Christ followers displayed miracles that saved, delivered, healed, and set people free! Holy Spirit would strengthen, move through, and minister boldness to Christ's followers.

In week 2, we learned how God indwells His people as a permanent resident for those who know Christ. Triune God has supreme control and sovereignty over the supernatural and natural realms. The kingdom of darkness creates confusion and chaos for us, and God's Spirit acts as a rudder and helper, guiding us to stay the course until final redemption.

Week 3 shared about the fellowship of God and how He indwells, pours out His Spirit, and has post-conversion encounters with His people. God is also sanctifying and transforming His people daily. In recapping, we recognize a theme surrounding God's power and authority. We cannot manifest a move of God; all we can do is respond as we live surrendered to Him.

Week 4 aims to teach you how to participate alongside the mighty move of God's Spirit and what that looks like for you in this season. I define "surrender" as a humbling of the soul desperate to be with God and deliberate to do what He asks. We understand the desperation; let's dive into the concept of deliberation.

Manifestations of Holy Spirit

In the apostle Paul's letters (often called the Pauline Epistles), he wrote about the Christian faith, what it means to be a follower of Christ, and how the Spirit manifests in and through God's people. **God's Spirit manifests character inwardly; His power moves outwardly and leads us through various ministry roles and tasks.** Paul boldly embraced the Spirit's ministry in a hurt world. He rebuked lies (Acts 13:9–12), delivered from demonic activity (16:16–24), and healed the sick and diseased (28:8–10). Paul also displayed godly character; for example, he displayed joy by praising God while being locked in jail (16:22–25), gentleness as he respectfully engaged different cultural beliefs in his preaching (17:1–34), and faith during a violent storm at sea (27:21–26). His ministry was marked by a display of God's Spirit inwardly and externally.

Understanding his ministry in Acts and his personal experience and revelation from God (Gal. 1:12; Eph. 3:3–5), we can trust Paul's words about the different manifestations of the Spirit and how the Spirit's ministry impacts us. Looking at Paul's words in 1 Corinthians 12:4–7, we see a variety of gifts (v. 4), services (v. 5), and activities (v. 6) that are given by the same Spirit. God's Spirit also empowers these manifestations in everyone (v. 6) and is for the building up of the church (see figure 13 starting on page 152).

As Holy Spirit dwells within, His sanctifying work makes us look more like Him. Both the holy work of developing fruit and the mighty move of the Spirit bring the fullness of Christianity into your life. As those called to serve do just that, they experience God. As you take on different tasks and activities for God, you strengthen the church and demonstrate

Him to your community. When we acknowledge Holy Spirit, the way He's inviting us to participate in our world, and embrace His power, we're walking out the abundant life Christ gave us.

Deliberate Participation

I was invited to an interdenominational women's conference where I was asked to teach the Bible and lead a ministry time afterward. The event lasted two days. On the first day, none of my books were sold at the book table, and no one was interested in my free online classes. *I pretend this is how the Lord keeps me humble.* My ministry partner and I snuck away for prayer on the second day. She prayed over me, and we asked that the Lord would lead our time and impact those present. I remember ending the prayer feeling a deep heaviness come upon me, and I said, "God, nothing else matters except You. Have Your presence invade our reality. Do what You want." As the women ate a meal together in the other room, my friend and I walked around the sanctuary, touching the chairs and praying for God to reach these women.

Thirty minutes later, I stood on the platform and shared a sermon on God's glory. One of the flaws of speaking after a meal is the battle for nap time begins. As I taught exegetically from the text, these faith-filled women looked right back, expressionless. I'd get an occasional smile or head nod here and there. Nothing is worse than a crowd you can't read. I was pretty sure I wasn't making a dent in their spiritual growth. I closed the teaching portion and moved into ministry.

> As Holy Spirit dwells within, His sanctifying work makes us look more like Him.

With various denominations represented, I explained how we wanted to provide opportunities for people to experience God and what that might look like. I invited anyone who wanted to repent and give their life to Christ or recommit to come to the altar. I also invited anyone who wanted greater freedom or a miracle to join us. Now, this isn't always the normal way I close a service. But the event coordinators recognized many of the women in the room were in a place of desperation, needing a touch from heaven.

The ministry time felt electric. Women began to *deliberately* move forward as they responded to the pull from God's Spirit. Holy Spirit ministered through our time. A word of knowledge was given from a woman who *deliberately* opened her mouth. She asked a woman if she had a specific medical condition. Looking shocked, the other woman confirmed the word was accurate, and we were able to pray specifically. As we *deliberately* prayed for another woman, we physically felt heat come from our hands, and the power of God moved her to tears as she acknowledged His power. It was the type of cry that hurt so good. As she *deliberately* kneeled to the ground, she didn't rush to get up but received whatever healing God had for her. There were countless stories like this from those meetings.

One woman encountered God in her seat as someone boldly leaned over and whispered, "The Lord wants you to know He sees you, your situation, and He is not finished yet." Emotional, she revealed, even though she'd been praying, she felt hopeless and at the end of the rope over a specific circumstance that had yet to be resolved. This was the encouragement she needed to endure. Months later, I received word those attendees are still talking about all the Lord did that weekend and how Holy Spirit was deliberately ministering specifically to the hearts of His people!

It was evident God had been moving from the beginning of the event-planning process. God encouraged the ministry leaders to plan and dream about this conference. The worship team was anointed to lead and serve joyfully; those welcoming people into the venue wore bright smiles and a friendly attitude. From the tech team to those cleaning the toilets, we all did our tasks, got out of the way, and God met us there.

I'm sharing adventures from my life as a minister, but we all know God isn't confined to a church building or Christian event! You can minister at church, in a conference room, in a classroom, or in a car. You can bring peace as you pray for a sick friend, proclaim faith to a weary coworker, boldly love your son's bully at school, and share encouragement with your daughter as you drive to the bookstore.

As I've stood on stages and behind pulpits, I can tell you the moment of impact does not start in the public place. Your private-time moments with God empower your public ones. This is where your relationship grows as you learn to trust the voice that is calling you close. God meets us in between the seen and unseen places too. In the hallway, in conversations on the way to the bathroom, joking between bites of breakfast, and sweet prayers as we say goodbye in the parking lot—God's Spirit is positioning you for purpose!

Godly Virtue and Spiritual Gifts

The world is filled with brokenness, beauty, and everything in between. As Christ followers, we are equipped to endure through the squiggly paths this world affords us in our lives. Because of God, our paths become straight and begin to make sense. We know through His Spirit, He gives us help, guidance, power, and a greater perspective toward His will as we walk with purpose. **God's Spirit moves within us by developing godly virtue and ministers through us with spiritual gifts.** It's mind-blowing to think how they are imparted to us!

We must remain humble and say yes to the areas God invites us into. There's an obedience God asks of those who know the good news. The practice of Christianity should be one filled with activity. In the book of Acts, we see it isn't just showing the acts of God's people but also the actions of God Himself. He's a loving God who draws people close through the power of the Spirit so they may truly live.

Pause and Reflect

When was the last time you were deliberate to cooperate with God's Spirit? What was the outcome? When we slow down to reflect on the ways God is leading us, we also get to remember how His goodness follows our obedience.

Daughters Arising

I parent my kids through the lens of understanding their potential. For example, last week one of my kids, who will remain nameless, said they had already fed the dog. The food was a day old, and the water was dirty. My child's yesterday deliberation was not helping today's situation. "I know you have it in you to clean the bowl and put out fresh food." Begrudgingly, my child took the crusty bowl, did what was asked, and the dog was impacted for the good. We parent by understanding our children's innate talents, skills, and abilities and by seeing their potential. I can only imagine God has molded us with such a perspective.

Think about this: What I did yesterday for God may impact me today, but you can't call it deliberate daily obedience. We aren't living truly surrendered if we're living from last year's activity. God sees the complete picture, knows our innate talents (after all, He gave them to us), gives us gifts, sees the beginning from the end, and provides us with fresh vision and purpose. God speaks to our potential all the time. As He speaks to our potential, this can be intimidating because we're only positioned in the right now and can't see the full picture. But what if …

What if women—interdenominationally across the Christian faith—rise to the potential of who God is inviting them to be and what He's asking them to do? This rising up isn't synonymous with "living our best life" or having success that impacts the world, so we're glorified. This rising up is a trust fall into God's arms. Can we trust Him daily?

In Luke 8:40–56, we read two powerful accounts of healing during Jesus' earthly ministry. The first is often referred to as "the woman with the issue of blood." The second healing account is of a man's dying daughter. The woman and father had a desperation to be with God and He responded with His power. Upon bringing resolution, Jesus said, "Child, arise" (v. 54). What if we, too, took those words to heart?

We live for God because He is worthy to be worshipped with this one precious life we've been given. He's worthy of it all—not half our time, resources, or attention. He's worthy of our lives being laid down daily as we live fully for Him. The beauty of a life laid down for God is that He equips us to be deliberate and strategic. We have everything we need to steward whatever He asks of us.

Fire marks those who touch it, and with one touch from God's Spirit, we're empowered to rise.

Spotlight of the Week

Figure 13. Manifestations of the Spirit
Thirty ways God ministers in and through His people by developing fruit, ministering with spiritual gifts, and empowering for service in ministry and activities that strengthen the church

| **Fruit of the Spirit** |
| **Power Grid:** Galatians 5:22-23 |
| The living presence of Holy Spirit within believers produces godly character. |

Fruit	Example	Fruit	Example
Love	Luke 6:27-28, 35	Joy	Acts 8:39; 16:34
Peace	Luke 8:48; Acts 9:31	Patience	Luke 8:15; Acts 26:3
Kindness	Acts 28:2	Goodness	Luke 6:45; Acts 11:24
Faithfulness	Luke 16:10; Acts 11:24	Gentleness	Matt. 11:29; Luke 18:16
Self-control	Acts 24:25		

Spiritual Gifts
Power Grid: 1 Corinthians 12:4-11; 27-31; Romans 12:3-8
Holy Spirit graciously and freely gives a gift and ministers powerfully through believers for the edification and equipping of the church.

Gift	Example	Gift	Example
Word of wisdom	Luke 2:40, 52; 21:15; Acts 6:3, 10	Word of knowledge	Luke 1:77; 2:15; Acts 8:20; 10:1-6
Prophecy	Luke 1:67; Acts 19:6; 21:9	Faith	Luke 8:48; 17:5, 19; Acts 3:16; 6:5; 11:24; 14:9; 16:5
Gifts of healing	Luke 4:40; 7:22; 8:2; 22:51; Acts 3:6-8; 5:16	Working of miracles	Luke 4:36; 6:19; 8:46; 9:1; 10:19; 21:26-27; Acts 2:22; 4:33; 10:38; 12:6-16; 19:11
Distinguishing between spirits	Luke 9:37-43; Acts 5:1-11; 16:16-18	Speaking in various kinds of tongues	Acts 2:4; 10:46; 19:6
Interpretation of tongues	Acts 2:6-11; 10:46		

Service in Ministry

Power Grid: 1 Corinthians 12:5, 28; Ephesians 4:11-16; Romans 12:6-8
Holy Spirit moves through a variety of roles in church ministry for those called to serve others.[2]

Service	Example	Service	Example
Apostles	Luke 6:13-16; 9:1-6; Acts 2:42-43; 5:12; 15:6; 2 Cor. 12:12	Prophets	Luke 2:36; 7:26; 11:49-50; Acts 13:1; 21:10
Evangelists	Acts 21:8; 2 Tim. 4:5	Shepherd/Minister	John 21:16-17; Acts 20:28; 1 Pet. 5:1-11
Teachers	Luke 2:46-47; 3:12; 7:40; Acts 13:1		

Activities

Power Grid: 1 Corinthians 12:6, 28; Romans 12:6-8
Holy Spirit moves through a variety of tasks as believers participate in the work of God.[3]

Activity	Example	Activity	Example
Helping	Luke 10:33-34; Acts 20:35	Acts of service	Luke 22:27; Acts 6:1-4
Administrating	Luke 8:3; Acts 15:25	Exhortation	Luke 3:18; Acts 15:32
Generosity	Luke 19:8; Acts 4:34-35	Leadership	Luke 22:24-32
Acts of mercy	Luke 10:30-37		

Day 1

IN SICKNESS AND IN HEALTH

How does God's Spirit minister healing?

*"Let all that I am praise the LORD; may I never
forget the good things he does for me. He forgives
all my sins and heals all my diseases."*

Psalm 103:2–3 (NLT)

Pray

Holy Spirit, help me testify that Christ is healer. Amen.

Read and Study Luke 8:40–56

With a dozen chronic conditions listed on my medical charts, my body still needs healing despite all the poking and prodding from ten different medical teams over the years. The impact has been far-reaching, robbing me of precious moments with my family and hindering my ability to fully engage in my work. Some days, I feel like a prisoner in my

Context Is Key

Before Luke 8:40, ten miracle accounts were recorded in Jesus' ministry. Luke 8:40–56 takes place in the region of Galilee in the middle of Jesus' power-filled ministry. Jairus, a synagogue leader, came to Jesus seeking healing for his dying daughter, while a woman with a bleeding issue did the same. The stories are written in a sandwich structure, often called *intercalated form*.[4] This means one story is inserted within the other and is frequently used to add insight or further the storyline.

body and struggle with all the underlying questions. *Are these symptoms connected to a bigger problem? Is this just aging? Why am I getting more questions than answers? If Jesus can heal, why isn't He healing me?*

Western civilization in the twenty-first century has endless ways to seek healing and wholeness for our bodies. Many methods and treatment ideas exist to get our body, mind, and soul aligned and healthy. But which ones can be trusted? What has a long-standing history of proven success? For example, a friend told me to put onions in my socks the other day to fight a cold. Two days later, I still had a horrible cold and had to add, "Why do my feet still smell like onions?" to my Wonder List (figure 6).

In this lesson, let's push aside the logic of modern medicine and wrestle through the mysteries of hard circumstances and what it means when we say, "God heals." After all, the theology of healing can be confusing, but it is worthy of conversation. Here are three truths to remember as we unravel the powerful work of God's Spirit through healing.

Truth #1

Jesus is Healer. The supernatural realm was threaded into every aspect of society in the ancient Mediterranean world. When one was sick, seeking healing through magic or divine miracles was not a foreign phenomenon. Shamans, priests, prophets, rabbis, Jewish sages, exorcists, magicians, sorcerers, and deities like Greek gods offered different healing methods than philosophers and medical practitioners. In the Gospels, a new type of healer emerged named Jesus.[5]

Jesus challenged the dominant religious and cultural beliefs, providing an alternative version of healing and salvation. Jesus' power came from Himself, not something He had to muster up. From the first century to the twenty-first, approaching Jesus as a healer holds significant implications for understanding the Christian religion and shaping society. Healer is who God is, and it's at the core of His identity. Jesus even commissioned His twelve disciples to walk in the same power and authority to proclaim God's kingdom and heal in His name (Luke 9:1).

Truth #2

Healing is an act that strengthens God's kingdom. There are eight more accounts in Luke of Jesus healing people until His death.[6] Crowds of sick people, people with leprosy, a concerned dad, and a blind man all approached Jesus and were met with healing. By examining the healing accounts in the Gospels, it's evident Jesus was widely recognized as a sought-after healer in Galilee and the surrounding regions.

As people went to Jesus for healing, they also encountered His teachings, a message of salvation, and His claim that He is the Son of God. This prolific healer's death, resurrection, and ascension only furthered His message of healing—both physically and spiritually. As people were healed by Jesus, the kingdom was expanding.

Truth #3

We participate in healing by approaching God. As we navigate our difficulties, we turn to God with the assurance His love and response will exceed our expectations. His response may not always be what we are initially searching for or how we imagine the outcome. However, it is in the approaching of Jesus that our relationship with Him is strengthened.

We may know these three truths to be theologically accurate, but the cries of the unhealed world needing a cure are a tension we live in daily. It's as if we're in the waiting room at the doctor's office. Some have found the remedy for the pain, and some sit in excruciating agony. It is not up to you if healing takes place in the form of an earthly miracle. I've found it's in the shaking of hard circumstances that we seek something to hold on to. From this place of desperation, God's Spirit ministers healing through Jesus as we reach for Him.

There are three "But Jesus" statements in Luke 8 following moments of tension that emphasize the importance of waiting for the full story (vv. 46, 50, and 52). God will finish the good work He has started in us. As we wait and wonder, we can cling to this hope even when we don't understand it. **I will always pray for instantaneous healing (unless told otherwise) and have faith that healing will come in one of four ways: in redemptive suffering, through a process (often with medicine or a medical team), in an instant miracle, or in kingdom come.**

You may be diagnosed with an incurable disease. But Jesus … You may be praying for your child to be healed from deep trauma. But Jesus … Your bestie may be struggling with mental illness. But Jesus … As we approach Christ in the natural, we can rest assured He will respond with the supernatural.

Question

After reading Luke 8:40–56, it's time to wrestle with it. How is Holy Spirit bringing revelation to your theology of healing?

Day 2

IN THE SECRET PLACE

How does spending time with God's Spirit in private change me?

"If you want a revival you have to pour your life out. That is the only way."[7]
Minnie F. Abrams, Methodist missionary in India, 1898

Pray

Holy Spirit, guide me toward being fully devoted to You. Amen.

Read and Study Luke 5:16 and Acts 1:14

I felt utterly powerless as I cried in my prayer closet the other night at 3:00 a.m. I'll be honest, my prayer closet was my bathroom floor—the only place in the house that felt private. For weeks, I had tossed and turned, finding little rest. I wanted to sleep; God wanted to orchestrate an encounter with a fresh perspective in the midnight hours. As life's circumstances unfolded and various challenges seemed to relentlessly bombard me, I found my safe place crumpled on the bathroom floor. Night after night I found solace fellowshipping with God.

Entering the bathroom late at night, I'd tuck away on the floor in my newly found safe place. I'd see my handwritten reminders with verses scribbled on the mirror declaring the goodness of God. I would pray, worship, and cry my face off. I would consider with the Lord why I was holding on to deep anger and resentment. I would ask Him why I was anxious or why a specific heartache was present.

In those vulnerable moments, void of pulpits or performance, I rediscovered the sacredness of the secret place with God. Perched on the ledge of the shower, nestled amongst the untidy presence of the clothes hamper and the toilet, I found comfort and contentment in God's presence. This went on for weeks.

One night in the bathroom-floor-secret-place, there was a distinct moment with Holy Spirit I'll never forget. I felt so ill that night that I could barely sit up. My prayer session was filled with sulking. I felt alone and wanted to be held and feel safe. Everyone in my household was sound asleep and would remain that way unless I started banging some pots and pans. And every mama knows you never wake a sleeping child (or husband for that matter)! Moving past the overly aggressive marching-band idea to get some company, I sat still in the waiting.

But God.

Tears streaming down my face, I whispered, "I have nothing left to give. Will Your power transform this situation? In my shortcomings, can Your strength be sufficient?" I was met with a godly power not even the greatest humans could muster.

As clear as day, in my inner spirit, I sensed the Lord firmly say, "No one will save you except Me."

It was one of those ouch realities that humbly reminded me I wasn't alone and refocused my perspective. God's transformative power was strengthening me in my weaknesses. The power of God came in and replaced my deep pain with loving compassion. I walked into the bathroom tormented with anger and loneliness and left transformed. I was filled and able to rise again. Everything changed, and I walked out of that bathroom a hundred pounds lighter. This moment was a spiritual marker that drew me into greater devotion to God. Even though I'd been a Christ follower for decades, I needed this filling from His Spirit.

The intentionality of these bathroom prayer sessions was not lost on me. It was as if the ashes of my soul were being blown upon, and the flame began to flicker once more. Night after night, I could feel God's tangible love and power fill me. I sat for hours praying and just being in stillness, welcoming Him to revive my soul.

The secret place and surrender are interwoven. The act of surrender empowers us to see our active God. Surrendering our schedule, agendas, distractions, ego, wants, and desires before the Lord empowers us to receive whatever He wants to pour out. In the surrender, we're emptied of the yuck and petitioning to be filled by more of God. In my case, I surrendered my self-reliant ways and was filled with a reminder of who does the saving. I pray we can be women who continuously surrender in the secret place.

Your secret place doesn't have to be the bathroom floor. It could be your car, your morning walk, or as you rock your grandbaby to sleep. During my kids' preschool years, my secret place was after they went to bed. I would sit next to Matt as he watched TV, put a blanket over my head, and pray. I know, my "tent days" sound silly. Last week, I was looking through my notebook from those prayer sessions, and let me tell you, God was there in that tent!

> Surrendering our schedule, agendas, distractions, ego, wants, and desires before the Lord empowers us to receive whatever He wants to pour out.

I've learned two greatest lessons from the secret place. First, your private moments with God shape and mold you for your public platforms. Holy Spirit shapes you with godly character and aids you to minister in His power! Maybe your public platform is being your kid's coach, a youth group leader, or on the board of directors of a local organization. Remember, your life is a ministry. As you step onto your platform, you shine bright, and as you step out of the public eye and into the shadows, God meets you and aids you in carrying out His mission.

Second and most important, your secret private moments with God are pivotal in getting to know Him. Void of distractions, you can thank God for who He is, pray for others, petition His promises, and find comfort as God's Spirit is present in your reality. Your secret place with

God empowers you to constantly live surrendered because you're reminded of who you're living for. He wants to meet with you! Can you make space to be with Him?

Questions

1. Luke 5 takes place during Jesus' earthly ministry. After He healed a man, verse 16 says, "Jesus often withdrew to lonely places and prayed" (NIV). Other translations say He went to "desolate places" (ESV) and would "withdraw to the wilderness" (NLT). Where can you go to withdraw and be with God? If you don't have a place, make time this week to create a cozy prayer corner, go on prayer walks, or find a place to be distraction-free with God.

2. Acts 1:14 takes place after the resurrection and before Pentecost. The text says the women, Mary, and others devoted themselves to prayer. What resulted from their devotion?

3. After receiving Holy Spirit, Christ followers devoted themselves to the apostles' teaching and the fellowship, to the breaking of bread, and the prayers (Acts 2:42). What does that devotion look like?

4. Read 1 Timothy 4:1. The greatest weapon against this type of deception is devotion to God. Have you or a loved one ever been devoted to the wrong things? What was the result?

5. How can you remain devoted to God in personal prayer? What can that look like in your current schedule? Put this into practice and reflect on how your time goes.

Day 3

IN THE SACRED CHURCH

How does Holy Spirit's ministry strengthen my church?

"This, then was the mission of the disciples: to be witnesses to the coming of the kingdom of God in Jesus, to carry the good news of the new exodus—of the new creation—to the ends of the earth, in the power of the Holy Spirit."[8]

Sean Gladding, *The Story of God, the Story of Us*

Pray

Holy Spirit, empower me with a gift of Your Spirit to serve my local church. Amen.

Read and Study Acts 18:26

God's Spirit empowers gifts in His people (1 Cor. 12:6), and He distributes them according to His will (1 Cor. 12:11; Heb 2:4). These supernatural gifts are word of wisdom, word of knowledge, prophecy, faith, gifts of healing, working of miracles, distinguishing between spirits, speaking in various kinds of tongues, and interpretation of tongues. You may sense one of these gifts is more prevalent in your life, but as you make yourself available, God can minister through any willing vessel as needed! In fact, Holy Spirit ministered all the gifts through Peter.[9] Perhaps that is what it means to live a Spirit-led life. We are women of tenacious faith, founded in the Word, and trusting God's Spirit to move.

May we be eager to receive the ministry of Holy Spirit within our lives. Let us reflect on the words Paul wrote to Christ's church, "Since you are eager for manifestations of the Spirit, strive to excel in building up the church" (1 Cor. 14:12). He went on to speak of orderly worship and echoed those sentiments, "Let all things be done for building up" (v. 26). The gifts from Holy Spirit are for the strengthening and edifying of the church!

> God's Spirit empowers gifts in His people, and He distributes them according to His will.

It is not for vain motivations we receive the Spirit's ministry. For example, you don't have a prophetic word—you believe Holy Spirit is ministering revelation through you. As we receive Holy Spirit's ministry, we're reminded these supernatural abilities are far from natural; they're a move of God. The words "supernatural gifts," "spiritual gifts," "sign gifts," or "manifestations of the Spirit" are often used interchangeably. As you witness using your gifts, people come to know Christ and grow in their relationship with Him. God's Spirit has been poured out, we are powered up, and people are pointed to Christ as His supernatural gifts reveal Him to the world.

In this lesson, we are getting a bird's-eye view of the gifts. The mention of charisma (gifts of the Spirit) is brief, but here's our focus: God's gift ministering through you strengthens the church. A power-filled church relies on God's Spirit, and a powerless church starts to rely on performance and status. Remain filled with the Spirit!

Together, let's prayerfully consider how we can participate in building a healthy, power-filled church community while growing in our gifts and godly character. Here are a few suggestions on how we do that:

- Become biblically literate (2 Tim. 2:15).
- Ask Holy Spirit for discernment and wisdom (1 Cor. 2:12–16).
- Recognize the fruit in yourself and others (Luke 6:43–45).

- Test everything and hold what is good (1 Thess. 5:21; 1 John 4:1–3).
- Repent and bear good fruit (Matt. 3:8; Acts 26:20).
- Rebuke false teachings (from self or others) and teach sound doctrine (Titus 1:9).
- Withdraw from the busy and spend time in prayer alone with God (Luke 5:16; 6:12–13).
- Lastly, go to church.

> A power-filled church relies on God's Spirit, and a powerless church starts to rely on performance and status. Remain filled with the Spirit!

Women are imperative in strengthening and sustaining God's church. We may not all serve the same function, tackle the same tasks, or have the same gifts, but we serve the same God. Lord, fan the flame in our families, friendships, and within our faith communities. May we walk in the maturity of knowing Christ. Pray Paul's words over yourself today:

> We will no longer be immature like children. We won't be tossed and blown about by every wind of new teaching. We will not be influenced when people try to trick us with lies so clever they sound like the truth. Instead, we will speak the truth in love, growing in every way more and more like Christ, who is the head of his body, the church. He makes the whole body fit together perfectly. As each part does its own special work, it helps the other parts grow, so that the whole body is healthy and growing and full of love. (Eph. 4:14–16 NLT)

Questions

1. Women were active in the early church, hosting, helping, teaching, prophesying, praying, and more. How was Priscilla ministering in Acts 18:26?[10]

2. In Acts 12:12 and 2 Timothy 1:5–6, we see God ministering through women as intercessors and through their legacy of faith. How have women of faith impacted your spiritual development?

3. After looking at the list of all the manifestations of the Spirit on pages 152–53, what stands out to you?

4. How do you see God moving in and through you or your family in this season?

5. In what ways do you see Holy Spirit active in and through your local church community? How can you contribute to fostering a healthy church environment?

Day 4

IN SURRENDERED PARTICIPATION

Where can God use me?

"The essence of discipleship is humility before God. That humility expresses itself as self-denial. Taking up the cross daily and following Jesus means approaching ministry in the world as he did.... The Savior bore rejection and death for others, and the disciple must follow in the same path of service."[11]

Darrell L. Bock, *Luke*

Pray

Holy Spirit, direct me to walk in Your ways today. Amen.

Read and Study Acts 2:42–47

Sitting on my table were three little bottles filled with sand. My daughter, Zoey, and her besties had made crafts earlier in the week and wrote encouraging notes. They decided to gift three bottles to me as well. I was touched by their thoughtfulness and tucked the bottles away, saving to read what was inside for later.

I opened one as sand poured onto my hand. I let it cascade onto the floor, mingling with the pile of dirty laundry that had accumulated there. I then unraveled the scroll that was smushed within. The handwriting was instantly familiar. Zoey, then age ten, had written in blue cursive, "Mom, you're the best mom ever. I love you so much. You're wonderfully and purposely made by God! —Zoey."

Tears welled up in my eyes. It was a simple and sweet moment. Holy Spirit ministered through Zoey with an exhortation from her written words. As I took it all in, I felt refreshed and encouraged. God used my kindhearted girl to pick me up. My weary soul held her God-breathed words for the remainder of the day, and the note still sits on my office shelf today.

We tend to overcomplicate spiritual gifts, misunderstand service roles within church ministry, and undervalue our activities, tasks, and function in the church body. God can use a person of any age as He empowers the tasks of His people as we help, live generously, lead confidently, exhort others, and display acts of service and mercy. Holy Spirit can empower these activities as you volunteer in your local church, impact your community, and go about your day-to-day business. These activities can also work alongside spiritual gifts, talents, and service within the church.

There was a time I was on bed rest during pregnancy due to preeclampsia. My mom showed up daily to watch my then toddler and help me with things around the house. Being on the receiving end, she displayed acts of service, joy, and generosity as a daily demonstration of the love of God.

On another occasion, two kindhearted souls spanning a distance around the globe volunteered to help with administrative tasks and odds and ends to support our ministry efforts. They gave their time and intercession for a year, and they've been a gift to my life ever since.

> God can use a person of any age as He empowers the tasks of His people as we help, live generously,

> lead confidently, exhort others, and display acts of service and mercy.

Recently, a friend had been on my heart for days. I ran into her at a school function and told her I'd been thinking of her and wondered if she was okay. She revealed a major crisis in her life, and after sharing, we prayed. I later repented. I realized I had missed these supporting tasks days earlier. Was Holy Spirit trying to minister through me, and I was oblivious? When I feel depleted, distracted, or consumed with myself, it feels hard to embrace the tasks God is inviting me to. Yet, in God's faithfulness and our repentance, we return to Him and get to try again.

Developing virtuous character and spiritual gifts, serving in church, and tackling Holy Spirit–led tasks—this is how we carry kingdom impact. This, too, is how we grow in intimacy with our Creator. It can feel underwhelming at times, though. Boldly embracing God's Spirit doesn't always mean it'll be extravagant. **I want the big, grandiose moments that feel weighty and substantial. But as I've walked through the refining fire of suffering, I've learned God is also at work in the small and mundane. Wherever God has you is where you need to be.**

In the moments when we show up for a goodnight kiss to our child and a whisper of "God loves you," God is planting seeds of endurance in the younger generation. Or when we are grocery shopping, slow down and notice the exasperated young mama juggling a gaggle of kids. In your offering of a supportive smile and a nod, God shows another sister she is seen and not forgotten. As you tackle that to-do list at work and make what feels like the millionth phone call, God's Spirit ministers through your joy-filled banter and gentle spirit. In the slowing down, God offers deliberate care as we tend to others and let them tend to us. Isn't this what living is all about? We see others, are being seen, and are walking with the Spirit of God.

One of my favorite passages on the early church is found in Acts 2:42–47 because it shows the many ways Holy Spirit ministers in the church. The early church exemplifies a powerful church, and we can do the same! Walk in your functions, your tasks, and your spiritual gifts.

Receive Holy Spirit manifesting good things through you. When you do, it's as if your soul settles and says, "This is what I was made for." It's a step closer to God. In God's presence, adoration is all our soul clings to. Even when life feels broken, may we still worship the One who makes everything beautiful. As missionary and author Elisabeth Elliot said, "The secret is Christ in me, not me in a different set of circumstances."[12] God is using you right where He's placed you.

I pray we find fulfillment in doing what God asks of us and we consider His to-do list worthy of our most valuable time. I pray His things come first, not last, and we aren't begrudgingly holding on to our agendas but fastening to His. I pray we can trust God's Spirit to minister through our demonstration of faithfulness as we show up in the messes, the mundane, and within the most beautiful of ways. In mundane and larger-than-life tasks, God's Spirit ministers through us, impacts others, and draws us closer to Himself.

May we pray our local church communities, however expressive in the gifts, embrace a mighty move of God. You are a piece of the church body. Your voice, spiritual giftings, service in ministry, and activity in the body of Christ are vital. The Helper is ready, waiting, and wanting to minister hope, healing, and reconciliation through a willing participant. I'm not asking you to make street preaching or demon slaying your full-time job; I mean, if the Lord wills it, why not? But I'm simply posing the question: Why not walk in the power of the Spirit and trust that God knows what He's doing?

Why not you? You have all you need—Holy Spirit.

Questions

1. In Acts 2:42–47, in what ways was God ministering through His people? What was the result of the Christ followers being used in this way?

2. In both big and small ways, how have you seen God using others to minister to you or your family? What was the result?

3. What is your spiritual gift (figure 13)? How have you tried to operate in the gift as you received the ministry of God's Spirit? Was it aligned with the biblical boundaries of Scripture?

4. In hindsight, have you ever missed an opportunity from Holy Spirit to support another?

5. How do you see God inviting you to participate in strengthening your local church? If you have yet to find a Bible-teaching church community, make it a point to attend a church service this weekend.

Day 5

IN THE STANDSTILL

What if I don't have my happy ending on this side of eternity?

"Through the agency of the Holy Spirit, the entire cosmos eventually will be brought into conformity with the rule and reign of Jesus Christ, to the eternal praise and glory of God the Father."[13]

Timothy C. Tennent, *Invitation to World Missions*

Pray

Holy Spirit, thank You for bringing deeper wisdom of the triune God and Your love for me. Amen.

Read and Study Acts 28:23–31

Tired of my broken body, I sent an SOS to our prayer team. My physical ailments were heightened heading into a full weekend of Bible teaching. The brain fog was thick, my mind was in a continuous race, and I was battling nausea that often came alongside some imbalanced hormones during that time of the month. *If you know, you know.* At the event, I asked some of the local ladies from the church to pray for peace over me as well. The intercessors gathered, and well, the fire of God fell. I don't know how else to describe it, but I physically felt God's power shoot through my head down to my toes. It was a physical sensation I never want to forget. It was like a fever raging through my body in a split second, leaving me with that tingly feeling you get when your foot falls asleep. After sitting in this moment for what felt like hours (yet it was a few minutes), I got up off the ground and had complete peace and clarity—the physical symptoms were gone. God was empowering me to pour out the message I had been called to preach.

A few minutes later, a friend and ministry partner came over and whispered to me that she had been approached by a woman named Olivia, standing beside her now, who was in heart failure and had been in and out of the hospital. The music had started; the event was beginning.

"I never do anything like this. Can you pray for me?" Olivia spoke softly with a stoic demeanor.

"Of course," I responded. "How do you want us to pray?"

"That I end well," she simply said.

The gospel of Luke ends with Jesus telling His disciples to wait for the Promised Presence. They waited well. Acts also ends with waiting. In Acts 19:11, Luke wrote, "God was doing extraordinary miracles through Paul." We've read of Paul's conversion and his adventures. From setting people free to raising the dead, God used him and other disciples to spread the gospel and strengthen the church. After more persecution and a shipwreck, Paul was in Rome with restrictions while continuing to boldly share the gospel (28:30–31).

At the end of Acts, there's no resolution on Paul's final verdict in Caesarea; he's in waiting. His journey in Acts ends under house arrest, and although the message of Christ is expanding thousands of miles, it has yet to go to the ends of the earth.

Acts is unresolved and abrupt because I believe modern-day Christians are walking out a proverbial Acts 29. From the first to the twenty-first century, all Christ followers are living out the last part of Acts 1:8. Believers are gifted an opportunity to embrace the indwelling of Holy

Spirit, receive His power, and respond as Christ's witnesses. There's a mission to take the gospel to the ends of the earth to expand on the work that Peter, Lydia, Paul, and the other Christ followers started.

Just as Paul's story was unresolved, so is mine. I haven't found the cure for all my health concerns. I'm still praying for healing and resolution to a situation that's been hurting my heart for years. A friend waits for a new job, a woman from my small group faces a hard adjustment in her family, and my greatest unresolve is joyfully found within the beauty of parenting. Matt and I are raising up Max and Zoey and cheering them on while they grow into all God has for them.

What beautiful and broken "unresolves" do you sit with today? **This book may be concluding, but our story with God is midsentence. Even in the unresolved, we are women who resolve to see His Spirit move.**

> There's a mission to take the gospel to the ends of the earth to expand on the work that Peter, Lydia, Paul, and the other Christ followers started.

The research for *The Promised Presence* started with the question, "Where is Holy Spirit in a world that hurts like hell?" As Matt and I chatted through the hard areas of our lives, he posed a question to which I now ask you—"What if you don't get the happy ending *you're* hoping for?"

I know I'm not the only one facing hardship.

In what we've processed together through Luke and Acts, all I ask is that you take your circumstances, both beautiful and broken, and search for God. Remember the key character traits we learned of Him. **Holy Spirit is promised to you, and God's Spirit will always point you to Christ. Look to Him!**

Vulnerability, prayer, and local church community are pivotal within the enduring of the saints. As my friend and I prayed over the woman with the heart condition, I was reminded we aren't in pursuit of a happy life. Although following God does bring ultimate happiness, the goal of this whole thing is that He is glorified and enjoyed until our own glorification as we're fully united with Him.

I don't remember the specific words we prayed over Olivia. All I know is at the end of the prayer, she went back to worship, and I ran to the bathroom. I sobbed beside the toilet over the woman who modeled a tenacious faith in the face of physical death.

> Vulnerability, prayer, and local church community are pivotal within the enduring of the saints.

Holy Spirit has been a topic of study for me for the past twenty-something years, and let me tell you, the Ministry of Desperation cannot be comprehended until a circumstance forces your hand. In our places of desperation, the ones where we face our deepest fears, oppression, and struggle through hardship, God ministers in real and personal ways. God's Spirit brings us into a place of holy comfort within the hard circumstances. Praying over a woman whose heart's desire is to finish strong, even with a broken heart, humbled me at the very core.

I love this quote from one of my favorite theologians, Sam Storms: "The power of God doesn't enable us to escape hardship and persecution but strengthens us to endure it without giving way to compromise or cowardice!"[14] We are courageous women who know that waiting and going are one and the same with the Lord. We can be still before God yet living on mission with Him. He will finish what He started.

In the meantime, God has given us a helper. Holy Spirit is an active part of your daily life and is shaping your worldview to encounter a miraculous God. Your hard circumstances are already in the Lord's hands and have found resolution. And He is with you in the mundane things in life, empowering you to endure. You are a model to those around you as you wait well. You don't need to literally go to the ends of the earth to preach the gospel; you need to go to the end of yourself. Look past yourself and see those placed in front of you. Not only can you show the love of Christ to others, but you can also receive love and compassion from others doing the same. Community is vital!

Keep moving in the waiting. You have the knowledge of His authority to walk in His power. God is faithful; He is sovereign, good, and a miracle-working God. God's presence is in your present reality. You are more than equipped to live a life of integrity that impacts your family, friends, and church community. You are more than equipped to live a life of purpose that is positioned toward Him. You are more than equipped to walk led by the Spirit as His gifts point people to Christ. Remember, you aren't the savior of the world; we get to worship the One who is! Praise God! God is close. What if *that's* the happy ending?

> We are courageous women who know that waiting and going are one and the same with the Lord. We can be still before God yet living on mission with Him.

Questions

1. In today's study scripture, Acts 28:23–31, what was Paul testifying?

2. How did people respond? Have you seen people respond in similar ways (Acts 28:24–25)?

3. Even though Paul was in a season of waiting, how do you see Holy Spirit at work in his life?

4. How do you see Holy Spirit at work in your life?

5. We are women focused in to see a present and personal God, even during the waiting! Consider all you've learned in *The Promised Presence*. What are key character traits of God you want to take away from this journey?

How may I pray for you in your next steps? Visit www.jennyrandle.com/pray and submit your request!

BENEDICTION

"According to the riches of his glory he may grant you to be strengthened with power through his Spirit in your inner being, so that Christ may dwell in your hearts through faith—that you, being rooted and grounded in love" (Eph. 3:16–17).

WEEK 5 PRE-SESSION QUESTIONS AND TEACHING VIDEO

Community Connection

Start the discussion by sharing some "Yay God" praiseworthy moments from the week. Taking time to celebrate how you see God moving is pivotal in recognizing a God on the move.

Learning Theology

- This past week, we read about the powerful work of God's Spirit. Our "Spotlight" was on how Holy Spirit develops godly fruit in us, ministers spiritual gifts through us, empowers us for service in ministry, and fills us for a variety of tasks and activities. What stood out to you in this week's lesson regarding Holy Spirit?
- Do you have a secret space to go and meet with God? What is it like and how has meeting with God strengthened your thoughts about Him?

- In learning how people in the Bible participated in strengthening the church, how does this motivate or challenge you to do the same? Holy Spirit ministers spiritual gifts for the strengthening of the church. Have you ever seen Holy Spirit minister spiritual gifts through someone or yourself? Was it aligned with the grid (the biblical boundaries of Scripture)?

Watch Jenny's Lesson 5 Teaching: Walk by the Spirit

URL: davidccook.org/access

Code: Presence

Living Out Theology

- Jenny reminded us that walking with God's Spirit is how we press on in a world that is being redeemed. What does this mean for you?
- Read "Final Exhortation" together on pages 183–84. How are you discerning your next steps with Holy Spirit? Can you commit to remaining deliberate to keep in step with Him?
- See page 178, question 5. Let's end by celebrating the character of God and who He is! How has your view of Holy Spirit been shaped through *The Promised Presence*?

Prayer Team

Pray together right now! I pray this is a safe environment for you to feel comfortable praying together. If you're able, turn on some worship music in the background. Welcome Holy Spirit into your time and trust Him to minister through you with His gifts, power, guidance, and loving care as you seek encouragement over your sister-friends.

Final Words for the Group

Congrats, you finished *The Promised Presence*! Be sure to keep this book handy in case you need to reference the Common Questions section later. Since you dug into the theology of God's Spirit together, dare I suggest *Flash Theology* as your next group adventure! You Spirit-led ladies will go even deeper into theology without feeling like you're drowning. Visit flashtheology.com for more info!

FINAL EXHORTATION

I wrote *The Promised Presence* for the struggling, the weak, the women who wonder where God is and are desperate to see Him move. I wrote this book for the strong ones finding their voice: the mama bears, college students, church grandmas, and friends. I wrote this for you, my sister in Christ.

Biblical women who have gone before us paved paths down unfamiliar terrain. We often find ourselves, although walking in a different cultural context, carrying out their legacy of faith. There are Deborahs and Miriams among us prophesying the will of God to the lost. I see Priscillas teaching others with the full council of Scripture and Naomis mentoring with wisdom. The Hannahs are fervently praying, and Esthers are courageously walking in their calling. I see Tabithas being known for generosity, serving others, and walking in their gifts. Then there are the Mary Magdalenes, who are transformed by God's power and devoting their lives to following Him.

Christ walked in supernatural power and authority. We read of His miracles, mission, and how the early church was strengthened as His Spirit was poured out. As you are desperate for Christ, remain deliberate to keep in step with His Spirit as you live in the fullness of knowing God.

Whatever your initial reasons for reading this book, I pray God answers your questions or deep longings in your soul. Most importantly, take everything you've learned in this book and place it under the authority of Scripture and the character of Christ.

We are theologians, mentors, advocates, warriors, intercessors, gifted, and firecrackers whose light cannot be contained. Holy Spirit is equipping us to walk filled with God's love and compassion, regardless of our circumstances or title. Receive the ministry of His Spirit and welcome God Himself in continually. Remain confident. God is good, and His Spirit is equipping you with the power to be a witness as the gospel goes to the ends of the earth! Raise your kids into the truth of who God is, share God's love with your neighbors and enemies, contend for freedom for your family, remain battle-ready and diligent to see the good, and step into your giftings. Keep going—testify with your life, actions, deeds, and words that Jesus is Lord!

Bonus Material

COMMON QUESTIONS

For the Theologians: What is the role of the Spirit in the Old Testament believer?

In doing an Old Testament (OT) survey about God's Spirit, one finds great depth in understanding who this person of the Trinity is. Holy Spirit isn't biblically confined within the New Testament's twenty-seven books from Matthew to Revelation. The Spirit of God was hovering over the waters in the creation account, as told in Genesis 1:2, all the way to God ministering prophetically through Malachi, and announcing the coming of the messenger who would prepare a way for the coming Lord (Mal. 3:1). Grasping this knowledge is essential to fully understand the New Testament (NT) early church. Holy Spirit didn't just pour out at Pentecost in Acts 2; He was active at the beginning of days, which is evident in the biblical timeline. **As we study how God moved, we expect a continual move of the Spirit.**

God created a lifesaving plan to rescue people from a desolate yearning to define what is true and morally correct, guiding them away from the pitfalls of personal autonomy. Adam and Eve's disobedience in the Garden of Eden is where this problem originated (Gen. 3). The identity of humanity strayed from being God's people, leaving them homeless from their place in paradise and separated from God's presence. Can you see how the power and promise of God's Spirit were pivotal in the life of Old Testament believers? God was preparing the path for the promised redemption!

The Spirit's character is the same throughout Genesis to Revelation. However, the name for the Spirit is not. The specific term "Holy Spirit" appears only three times (Ps. 51:11; Isa.

63:10, 11). In many cases, the word "Spirit" occurs in combination with the divine name—the Spirit of God, the Spirit of Yahweh, the Spirit of the Lord.

The Spirit came upon Old Testament believers to empower them to tackle the assignments God asked of them. Holy Spirit clothed Judge Gideon with empowerment for deliverance (Judg. 6:28–35), rushed upon King Saul to kindle his anger (1 Sam. 11:1–15), and came upon prophet Isaiah as the Lord anointed him with authority for the work of ministry (Isa. 61:1). Other accounts show God's Spirit filling people with power (Mic. 3:8), coming on (1 Sam. 19:20), and rushing upon the believers (1 Sam. 9:6). Our New Testament language would describe this as a "filling" of the Spirit.

Holy Spirit was filling leaders for their tasks, and He was promised to be poured out on all people. Bezalel, the chief craftsman, was filled with God's Spirit to work on the Tabernacle (Ex. 31:3). God filled Saul as the Spirit of God rushed upon him with prophetic words before his role as king over Israel (1 Sam. 10:10). Elizabeth was filled with Holy Spirit while pregnant with John the Baptist (Luke 1:41). Holy Spirit was also promised as Ezekiel and Joel prophetically shared with the people of Israel that the Spirit would be put within and poured out to all people (Ezek. 36:26–27; Joel 2:28–29).

Figure 14. Old and New Covenant Events with God's Spirit
Biblical theology shows that God's Spirit was promised, and filled, baptized, and indwelled His people

Old Covenant		Covenant Shift Life of Jesus		New Covenant (after the Lord's Supper in Luke 22:20)			
→		→		→			
Ex. 31:3 1 Sam. 10:10 Luke 1:41	Joel 2:28–29	Luke 3:16 Luke 11:13 John 14:17	Luke 3:21–22	Luke 24:49 Acts 1:4, 8	Rom. 8:9	Acts 2:4 Acts 10:44–45 Acts 19:1–10	Acts 4:8 Acts 13:9 Acts 13:52
Filling	Promise	Promise	Baptism	Promise	Indwell	Baptism	Fill

The role of God's Spirit in the life of the old covenant believer points people to the new covenant promise. As stated earlier, the Spirit empowers leaders to prophesy. Joel 2:28–29 reads, "And it shall come to pass afterward, that I will pour out my Spirit on all flesh; your sons and your daughters shall prophesy, your old men shall dream dreams, and your young men shall see visions. Even on the male and female servants in those days I will pour out my Spirit."

This same Spirit is revealed to rest upon the Messiah as the new covenant is enacted (Isa. 11:1–16; 42:1–9). The Messianic promise is connected to the power and pouring out of the Spirit. The foreshadowing in Isaiah 32:15–18 is a reminder of the coming kingdom.

After the Lord's supper in Luke 22:20, we read accounts of Holy Spirit fellowshipping in new ways that were previously promised (Luke 24:49; Acts 1:4, 8). In Romans 8:9, Paul shared how God's Spirit lives in all believers. Many refer to this as God's Spirit "indwelling believers." There are accounts of Holy Spirit baptizing believers (Acts 2:4; 10:44–45; 19:1–10) and filling people for their tasks (Acts 4:8; 13:9; 13:52). The new covenant enacted the plan of salvation and was fulfilled through the life, death, and resurrection of Jesus, and at Pentecost, the way God's Spirit dwelled with His people became permanent.

The OT establishes a pneumatology rich in depth toward understanding who the Spirit of God is. He restores, regenerates, strengthens, equips, prophetically enables, and promises to rest upon the believer. This knowledge is necessary for the NT early church and noteworthy for the end-days believers. This same Spirit transforms hearts, empowers for divine tasks, and has been poured to indwell the Christ follower. May the OT believers' journey bring us to remembrance; the rescue plan will be complete as restoration is found through Christ enabled by the Spirit.

For the Mentors: How can I help others hear and respond to Holy Spirit?

God speaks to us in several ways: through having a relationship with Jesus, within the Bible, through the church, as we worship and pray, through other people, within creation, and through the circumstances of our lives like dreams, visions, or personal situations.[1] Holy Spirit can move and communicate to you through any eight of those scenarios, but know anything God says will always align with His Word and character. **Everything God says will be backed by Scripture ... if it's not, it's not God.**

Often, some things hold us back from hearing God's voice. Sin, distractions, isolation, fear, and suffering are some common things that make us feel like we can't hear God. But rest assured, Holy Spirit is an active presence in Christ followers and wants to teach you how to discern His will and walk in His ways! Your relationship with God is *not* one-sided. If you're asking this question, "How does God speak?" read the Bible. This is the greatest way you'll hear Him as you invite God's Spirit to make the text come alive to you.

I wrote a book called *Getting to Know God's Voice: Discover the Holy Spirit in Your Everyday Life* (Harvest House, 2020). It's a 31-day interactive journey through understanding how to discern God's voice. You may find it a helpful resource if you're learning to listen.

For the Advocates: How do I pray for the sick?

In Scripture, we see Holy Spirit ministering through believers with the gifts of miraculous powers and healing. Demonized people were set free; others found spiritual healing through salvation, and healing from physical or mental ailments. Some were removed from isolation and welcomed into the community, and others were raised from the dead. But the question remains: How do modern-day Christ followers participate in praying for the sick?

My theory is simple: always pray for healing over a person, yourself included (unless told otherwise). Remember, sometimes healing can come in an instant, sometimes a process, but healing and wholeness will come for Christ followers (now on earth or in eternity). The great news is you do not have to have the gift of healing to pray for healing. Although God often ministers through those with the gifts of healing, He can minister healing through any willing vessel who has faith in Him as the Healer. Studying the clear direction in James's writings telling Christians how to live, my response about praying is based on his advice and what we've already learned in Luke–Acts.

Is anyone among you sick? Let him call for the elders of the church, and let them pray over him, anointing him with oil in the name of the Lord. And the prayer of faith will save the one who is sick, and the Lord will raise him up. And if he has committed sins, he will be forgiven. Therefore, confess your sins to one another and pray for one another, that you may be healed. The prayer of a righteous person has great power as it is working. (James 5:14–16)

Figure 15. Healed in Jesus' Name
Guidelines for praying for the sick and suggested scripture

Hands: Ask if you can touch or lay hands on the sick person (Luke 4:40; 13:13).

Empower: Trust Holy Spirit will embolden your words, give wisdom, and pour out His Spirit. Sometimes, healing and deliverance go hand in hand. Consider if you need to pray over someone for freedom.

Anoint: Church leaders can anoint the sick with oil in the name of the Lord (James 5:15).

Lead with Love: Follow Jesus' ministry model and lead with compassion. Be confident, too, because you have faith in Christ as a healer (James 5:15).

Express: If needed or the Lord urges this conversation, have the person privately confess sins (Acts 19:18; James 5:16; 1 John 1:9).

Declare: Read Bible verses over the person that declare God as healer. Praying biblical truth and God's promises is the greatest weapon to command sickness, disease, and strongholds to flee. **At the end of the prayer, declare with authority, "In Jesus' name, amen."**

Don't make this a legalistic ritual hoping to say the perfect verse so you'll "manifest miracles." You aren't like those ancient healers performing and can't manifest anything. Rather, pray as remembrance and celebration, trusting Holy Spirit to minister through you in whatever way He deems fit.

Pray This Way (Suggested Scripture)		
For Declaring Jesus as Healer Psalm 30:2 Psalm 103:2–6 Psalm 107:20 2 Corinthians 1:3–4	**For Physical Health** Psalm 46:1 Psalm 103:2–3 Jeremiah 30:17 John 10:10	**For Mental Health** Psalm 27:13–14 Psalm 34:17–18 Psalm 42:11 Psalm 139:13–14 Psalm 147:3 John 10:10 Philippians 4:6–7 2 Timothy 1:7 1 Peter 5:6–7
For Spiritual Health/ Salvation Psalm 51:10 Matthew 11:28–29 John 10:10 Romans 10:9–10 Ephesians 2:8–9 Hebrews 9:14 1 Peter 2:24	**For Freedom** Psalm 34:17 Psalm 118:5 Matthew 6:13 John 10:10 2 Corinthians 3:17 Galatians 5:1	

Remember, God is doing miracles as He heals someone in an instant, and as He sustains through sickness. Don't diminish or feel defeated in how God responds to your petition. Sickness and disease are not a gift from God but the reality of a broken world. We will battle against the broken, and we must always contend for a supernatural move of God in the natural! God's Spirit is with you as you do. The next time you casually tell someone you'll be praying for them, pause and ask if you can do it right at that moment. Together, approach God for healing and thank Him for comfort in the sustaining. Come alongside the person and make an appeal for sickness to flee in Jesus' name and pray for them to be fully healed and flooded with peace that surpasses all understanding as they encounter a fresh filling of Holy Spirit.

For the Warriors: How can I help others find freedom?

If you've found freedom in Christ, know that it isn't just for you. Freedom is for those you interact with too. I'm sure at one point you've wondered if you needed to cast a demon out of that crazy preschooler who was acting like a fool. *We've all been there.* I've found it's such a gift to speak to a person's potential.

One time, a friend was having a hard time with her teenage son. He was mad, furious. His rage affected the whole house with what could only be described as darkness. After chatting, I reminded my friend of the power to speak to his potential and declare God's truth! She began to speak Scripture over him and the situation. Everything changed. The atmosphere of the whole place shifted toward the kingdom of God.

We need the Spirit's perspective to remind us that even in our weakness, we're strengthened toward freedom. In Holy Spirit's companionship and advocacy, liberation comes as He rests within. Jesus gave His followers the authority to cast out demons and act under God's authority as church representatives. The apostles did not act arbitrarily or operate apart from Holy Spirit. There was God-found confidence to minister to those their paths came across.

There may be seasons when God leads you to be the facilitator of freedom, and other seasons when you are the receiver. This may look like multiple meetings with a trained leader or counselor at your local church. It may be responding at the altar in whatever way God's Spirit invites you to. Other times, it's simply God encountering you, and in a single moment, freedom is found.

In your quest for freedom, here are some quick and practical tips you can use to maintain a tactical offense against the enemy. When we systematize the supernatural, we make a move of God an event to be obtained rather than a God to behold. This is not a formula or checklist but a reminder to help you serve well. Most importantly, you have Holy Spirit inside of you guiding you day by day.

> When we systematize the supernatural, we make a move of God an event to be obtained rather than a God to behold.

Fill Up: Stay aligned with God through prayer. Study the Bible. Pray, fast, and remain alert and battle-ready by putting on the whole armor of God (Eph. 6:10–18). Trust Holy Spirit to mold your life to the likeness of Christ.

Clean Up: Repentance and vulnerability will move you past the enemy's lies, harmful addictions, an identity crisis, and so much more. Confess and repent of any sin, actively avoid temptation, forgive others, release bitterness, and practice self-control. Trust Holy Spirit to move within your life.

Power Up: Seek wise counsel, have accountability, remain in fellowship, participate in a local church, serve others, practice generosity, spend daily time with the Lord, and understand your giftings. Trust Holy Spirit to minister through your life.

Gather Up: As a leader, creating a comfortable environment for people to get uncomfortable to share their hardships is critical. Preserve this space at all costs. This, too, is vital for building kingdom connections and friendships. If you're hosting a prayer time, be prayed up before the gathering and have at least two leaders available to pray. Publicly share the group boundaries, and stick to them. Sometimes, finding freedom requires looking a little funny in the process. Discern between the work of the Spirit and a distraction from the enemy. **What is said in that room stays in that room. But what is imparted in that room will impact the world.**

Keep Up: Warfare may feel fragile, cause the temptation to isolate, or trigger shame to creep in. Continue to be encouraged (or encourage others if you're praying for them) that freedom is maintained. Continually keep the door closed to any harmful habits. This may require practical help like counseling or actively attending Bible studies. Freedom requires upkeep so the enemy doesn't return (Luke 11:11–26). One must be filled up with Holy Spirit in place of the thing they were delivered from. Your greatest asset is your church community, so keep up with those who love and want what's best for you.

For the Intercessors: Should I pray for Holy Spirit to fill others?

Yes, we should not shy away from praying for the filling and baptism with the Spirit. It is biblical, after all! God's Spirit is the promised gift (Luke 24:49; Acts 1:4–5). Here is the thing about gifts: one party gives, and the other receives. God's precious gift—the Holy Spirit—is available to believers, but we must ask, wait, and be ready to receive from God.

Four reasons why we should pray for Holy Spirit:

It's a Command: Jesus "orders" His disciples to stay and wait in Jerusalem for the promise of the Father, the Holy Spirit (Luke 24:49; Acts 1:4–5).

God's Continued Presence: Jesus spoke about the promise from the Father, but where did that promise originate? In John 14:16, 18, Jesus told His disciples, "I will ask the Father, and he will give you another Helper, to be with you forever.... I will not leave you as orphans; I will come to you." Jesus knew His earthly life was ending soon. Rather than abandoning His followers, Jesus promised the triune God's continued presence through the Trinity's third person.

Power: "I am sending the promise of my Father upon you. But stay in the city until you are clothed with power from on high" (Luke 24:49). Acts 1:8 reinforces that claim, "You will receive power when the Holy Spirit has come upon you, and you will be my witnesses in Jerusalem and in all Judea and Samaria, and to the end of the earth." The power comes first, followed by witnessing to the world. We need the Spirit's power to witness to the world well.

Unity: "For just as the body is one and has many members, and all the members of the body, though many, are one body, so it is with Christ. For in one Spirit we were all baptized into one body—Jews or Greeks, slaves or free—and all were made to drink of one Spirit" (1 Cor. 12:12–13). In other words, receiving the Holy Spirit unifies the diverse body of believers.

How to pray for Holy Spirit to fill others: *Father, thank You for loving us so much that You sent help through Jesus and Your Spirit. Thank You for the promise of Your Presence. We cannot fulfill Your commission on our own. I pray for a filling of Holy Spirit to abide in us and empower, instruct, and direct us to bring Your kingdom on earth as it is in heaven. Amen.*

For the Gifted: How do I operate in my spiritual gifting?

God has given you gifts. So, what do you do with them? How do church leaders manage this outpouring of God's Spirit so it isn't chaotic, weird, or manipulative? What if we, the church body, made three commitments together?

An active church is a powerful church for God. The areas God invites us into require a response of sacrifice and surrender from us. Again, we can be desperate to see God, but are we deliberate about doing what He asks? As you remain intentional about strengthening the church through manifestations of God's Spirit, I want to remind you of a few things.

Love speaks louder than any of the spiritual gifts (1 Cor. 13:2). As we are rooted in love, we will display spiritual gifts honorably and with integrity. We are to pursue both love and desire the gifts (1 Cor. 14:1). (What Paul shared with the Corinth church members can be applied to our modern-day churches as well.) **As Holy Spirit is present within, Christlike character is produced. As the ministry of Holy Spirit is received, the spiritual gifts reveal the truth of Jesus.** He is a God who sees, knows, and cares about individual circumstances and hearts. He is a God calling His people close and restoring us to wholeness.

The apostle Paul wrote, "Now there are varieties of gifts, but the same Spirit; and there are varieties of service, but the same Lord; and there are varieties of activities, but it is the same God who empowers them all in everyone" (1 Cor. 12:4–6). See figure 13 on pages 152–53 for a list and examples of the manifestations of God's Spirit. These are all ways we strengthen the church for the common good.

As you prayerfully discern what your spiritual gift(s) are, consider making these three commitments:

- Commit to studying the Bible to understand how God's Spirit manifests and what the gifts are.
- Commit to learning and growing, and eagerly manifest the gifts of the Spirit and display them with integrity and honesty.
- Commit to remaining humble and under pastoral and church leadership as the gifts are operating within your life.

We are all individual members that make up the body of Christ (1 Cor. 12:27). The gift of Holy Spirit gives all believers a gift. As you embrace your gift, you are helping the church body function to its whole capacity. Every member matters, which means you are a vital part!

For the Firecrackers: What does my authority look like as a Christ follower?

Luke used the Greek word *dynamis* in his gospel and in Acts, which means "power." ***Dynamis* was often associated with a supernatural reality that contained authority and strength.** Figure 16 demonstrates how Jesus' dynamis power is connected to healing and miracles. The healings done by Jesus were attributed to the power of Holy Spirit ministering through Him and His followers (Luke 9:1; 10:19; Acts 2:22; 19:11).

Figure 16. Acts 10:38 Power Linked to Other Scripture
Condensed lexicon link with "power" connected to healing and miracles

"[Peter recounts] how God anointed Jesus of Nazareth with the Holy Spirit and with **power**. He went about doing good and healing all who were oppressed by the devil, for God was with him." Acts 10:38					
Jesus returned in the **power of the Spirit** to Galilee. (Luke 4:14)	What is this word? For with authority and **power** he [Jesus] commands the unclean spirits, and they come out! (Luke 4:36–37)	As he [Jesus] was teaching, Pharisees and teachers of the law were sitting there, who had come from every village of Galilee and Judea and from Jerusalem. And the **power** of the Lord was with him to heal. (Luke 5:17)	And all the crowd sought to touch him [Jesus], for **power** came out from him and healed them all. (Luke 6:19)	Jesus said, "For I perceive that **power** has gone out from me." (Luke 8:46)	He called the twelve together and gave them **power** and authority over all demons and to cure diseases, and he sent them out to proclaim the kingdom of God and to heal. (Luke 9:1–2)

Jesus displays power when He calls people into repentance (Luke 10:13), commands spirits to come out (Luke 4:36; Acts 10:38), heals people (Luke 5:17; 6:19; 8:46), does signs and wonders (Acts 2:22), and returns in the second coming (Luke 21:26–27). Holy Spirit is this miracle-working power (Acts 1:8) who emboldens people to testify and share the gospel (Acts 4:33).

Even when Jesus was physically absent from earth (more specifically, when He was exalted and acting through His Holy Spirit), His apostles could simply say the name of "Jesus." His name alone carried enough authority and power to move a lame man to walk, leaving the witnesses amazed and prompting them to question the identity of this remarkable moniker (Acts 3:1–10). In all these situations, Holy Spirit ministered the dynamis power.

Another way God's Spirit ministered power is through Christ's followers. Instead of passively praying, they commanded healing rather strongly. From shaking off snake bites (Acts 28:3–6) to lifting the dead to life (Acts 20:10–12), there was an authority in action and voice with the followers of Christ.

Holy Spirit ministered healing through these believers' bold words:

- Peter—"In the name of Jesus Christ of Nazareth, rise up and walk!" Peter took him by the right hand and raised him up (lame healed, Acts 3:6–7).
- Ananias—"Brother Saul, the Lord Jesus who appeared to you on the road by which you came has sent me so that you may regain your sight and be filled with the Holy Spirit." And immediately something like scales fell from his eyes, and he regained his sight. Then he rose and was baptized (blind healed, Acts 9:17–18).
- Peter—"Jesus Christ heals you; rise and make your bed." And immediately he rose (paralyzed healed, Acts 9:34).
- Peter—"Tabitha arise." And she opened her eyes and Peter presented her alive (dead healed, Acts 9:40–41).
- Paul—Someone fell asleep while listening to Paul teach and fell out a third-story window. Lifting him off the ground, Paul said, "Do not be alarmed, for his life is in him." ... And he was alive (dead healed, Acts 20:10–12).

There are over ten accounts in Acts of Holy Spirit ministering through Christ followers and healing the sick. In every account—and where the stories are more generic or contain groups of miracles—there is always a Christ follower speaking boldly. Their ministry commands change for the good, rather than fluffy prayers to pacify a situation in the moment. They didn't need a Band-Aid to cover the wounds because they knew God's power cauterized the pain right at the source. This same power, given by the Spirit, is for believers today. You have the same authority as the disciples we've read about in Acts.

There's a compassion God has placed within you to love, honor, and serve others well. He's given you eyes to see the needs of others. You are not a second-class citizen in the kingdom of God. You are not too busy for God's business. Your role is vital to strengthening the church, your family, and your peer group. You, my friend, are not forgotten or overlooked. Your demeanor and disposition matter, so come out of hiding. God sees you; He is with you and has sent you a helper. Be emboldened! You have the authority to walk in strength, react in grace, and speak truth boldly, cauterizing hearts toward Jesus!

ACKNOWLEDGMENTS

Before we begin the slow clap for the people who have encouraged my faith and throughout writing *The Promised Presence*, I'd like to pause and praise the sustainer of such an endeavor. Thank You, God, for meeting me in my moments of despair and breathing life into dormant places. You've set a spark in my soul that I pray burns until my last breath.

Thank you to the mentors and friends who have shaped my faith in big ways:

Coach Kim Wilson—God used your invitation to church to change the trajectory of my life. Thank you for teaching me about Jesus and what it means to walk with God.

Mike Nagel—There are a lot of other places you could have been during our college years. But you patiently taught me the tenets of our faith and modeled it in ways I will never forget. Thank you.

Michelle Cuthrell and Brynn Shamp—Thank you for your ministry of authentic friendship, compassion, and fun.

Steph and Mark Schilling—Thank you for pastoring me and providing prophetic encouragement throughout the years.

To my family—Thank you for your support, I love you.

Matt, your faith strengthens me.

Max, your Hakuna Matata passion for the Lord inspires me.

Zoey, your worship ushers in a piece of heaven and moves me.

To the people who shared a piece of their story with us in these pages—Thank you for pointing us to Christ.

From the idea to its birth, this book has been a three-year labor of love and a dream long before that. It sure is a team effort! Steve Laube, thank you for guiding my writing career and finding places for my words to land. I'm grateful to the team of publishing professionals at David C Cook/Esther Press, Susan McPherson, Stephanie Bennett, James Hershberger, Susan Murdock, and Jack Campbell for using your God-given gifts and talents to strengthen the church body. I'm also thankful for the research of Paul Bullock and theological review by Brayden Brookshier.

To my past and present church families, thank you for inviting Holy Spirit to move amongst our midst and for walking in your gifts with integrity and might.

And to you, dear reader, thank you for reading these words. I pray we live them out together as we remain desperate for God and deliberate to do whatever He asks of us.

APPENDIX OF FIGURES

Figure 1. Understanding of Luke–Acts
- A comparison of Luke's writings in the Bible (page 21)

Figure 2. Godly Perspective in the Wondering
- How God brings calm in a world of confusion (page 39)

Figure 3. Stability in the Waiting and Wondering
- The transformation when human uncertainty converges with God (page 43)

Figure 4. Wonder List in the Gospel of Luke
- Documented miracles after Jesus' baptism (pages 47–48)

Figure 5. Pillars of Personhood
- Nine areas of focus for a purposeful life (page 52)

Figure 6. Wonder List in My Life
- Documented miracles unfolding in my story (page 55)

Figure 7. Wonder List in the Book of Acts
- Documented miracles in Acts (pages 59–60)

Figure 8. Promise-Keeping God
- Two promises that bookend the narrative in Luke (page 78)

Figure 9. The Clash of Kingdoms
- The structure of God's org chart and the supernatural battle in the natural world (page 88)

Figure 10. Biblical Witnesses on Mission
- Examples of the early church expanding as Christ is proclaimed (page 102)

Figure 11. Holy Spirit's Fellowship with Followers of Christ
- The relationship between God's Spirit and His people and three ways He interacts (page 113)

Figure 12. Receiving Holy Spirit and Church Growth
- Four biblical accounts of how, when, and the result of Spirit baptism (pages 122–23)

Figure 13. Manifestations of the Spirit
- Thirty ways God ministers in and through His people by developing fruit, ministering with spiritual gifts, and empowering for service in ministry and activities that strengthen the church (pages 152–53)

Figure 14. Old and New Covenant Events with God's Spirit
- God's Spirit was promised, and filled, baptized and indwelled His people (page 186)

APPENDIX OF FIGURES

Figure 15. Healed in Jesus' Name
- Guidelines for praying for the sick and suggested scripture (page 189)

Figure 16. Acts 10:38 Power Linked to Other Scripture
- A condensed lexicon link with "power" connected to healing and miracles (page 195)

GLOSSARY

Angelology—The study of angels.

Apostle—A person who serves in ministry that is sent out proclaiming a message. They act as a special messenger from God. In the New Testament, these individuals were appointed by Jesus or authorized and sent by other apostles to serve as foundation leaders, carrying out the mission of spreading the gospel and establishing the church. Apostles were often leaders of leaders, as seen when the apostles chose the deacons (1 Cor. 12:28; Eph. 4:11–16; Acts 6:1–7).

Baptism with the Holy Spirit—A onetime defining moment in which the empowering presence of the Holy Spirit becomes a tangible reality, actively immersing and shaping one's life. This moment is often equated to when the believer receives the Spirit and responds to His power, enabling one to walk in obedience to Christ (Luke 3:16; Acts 2; 8:14–17; 11:16).

Biblical Freedom—Liberation is found in Christ who brings freedom from the bondage and consequences of sin. Those who follow Christ are liberated from sin and death. Freedom is beyond a moral compass; it's a lifestyle of walking out the Christian identity (John 8:36; Rom. 6:22–23; 8:2; Gal. 5:13).

Biblical Theology—The study of specific themes and concepts in relation to the whole canon of Scripture and throughout the biblical narrative.

Biblical Worldview—A Christ-centered perspective that looks through the lens of the Holy Scriptures to interpret and shape one's morality, ethics, and view of the world.

Cessationism—The extraordinary manifestations of God's presence and power, as shared in biblical accounts, is restricted to a specific time and are no longer accessible or relevant to believers today. Those who hold this doctrine believe gifts like healing, distinguishing spirits, and speaking in tongues ceased in the apostolic age.

Continuationism—God is continuously involved in the lives of believers with the potential for ongoing miraculous experiences. Those who hold this doctrine believe the gifts of the Spirit continue and are for today.

Deliverance—Being saved and/or set free and liberated from captivity, harm, or the enemy's schemes demonizing or destroying your life. True deliverance is found in the God of the Bible (Isa. 61:1; Luke 4:18).

Demonology—The study of demons.

Discernment—The ability to recognize truth, lies, good, or evil and consider God's ways and guidance (Deut. 32:29; Prov. 14:8).

Disciple—The New Testament uses this term to describe a student and follower of Jesus Christ (Matt. 28:19; Luke 14:27; John 13:35).

Distinguishing between Spirits—When Holy Spirit gives the ability to discern or judge between supernatural beings. This is a gift given by Holy Spirit to believers for the strengthening of the church (1 Cor. 12:10).

Doctrinal View—A system of beliefs.

Eschatological Hope—Eschatology is the study of last things. This term refers to the expectation that Christ will fully restore creation in the end times. Christ followers will be with Him in eternity, which gives His followers a present-day purpose (1 Thess. 5:1–11; 2 Pet. 3:10; Rev. 11:15–19).

Evangelist—A person who serves in ministry as an evangelist is appointed to proclaim the good news of Christ and lead people into the Christian faith (Eph. 4:11–16).

Exegetical Teaching—A type of Bible teaching that typically goes line by line through a portion of Scripture and interprets the historical and cultural context of that day in order to uncover the original meaning.

Filling of Holy Spirit—The continuous experience of surrendering to Holy Spirit's influence and empowerment, resulting in transformation and alignment with God's will in a believer's life (Luke 4:1; Acts 4:31; 11:24; 13:52).

First-Tier Essentials—The fundamental truths relating to salvation in Christianity. These are the beliefs that make a Christian, a Christian.

Gift of Faith—Holy Spirit ministers a bold confidence and trust to believe. This is a gift given by Holy Spirit to believers for the strengthening of the church (1 Cor. 12:9).

Gift of the Interpretation of Tongues—When Holy Spirit gives the ability to make sense of a different language. This is a gift given by Holy Spirit to believers for the strengthening of the church (1 Cor. 12:10, 30).

Gift of Various Kinds of Tongues—When Holy Spirit gives the ability to speak in different languages. This is a gift given by Holy Spirit to believers for the strengthening of the church (1 Cor 12:10, 28).

Gifts of Healing—When Holy Spirit ministers divine repair to physical, mental, spiritual, or social areas needing restoration. This is a gift given by Holy Spirit to believers for the strengthening of the church (1 Cor 12:9, 28).

Glossolalia—A manifestation of the Spirit where someone speaks in tongues or a heavenly language (Acts 2:4; Rom. 8:26–27).

Holy Spirit—An active presence of God throughout the creation story to the completed story. Christ's followers have been given the gift of a Helper who transforms, guides, and empowers them as they endure in faith in a world being redeemed. He is a "He," not an "it." He is not a substance but the third person of the Trinity. He is co-eternal and co-equal to Father God and Lord Jesus (John 14:26; Luke 12:12; Acts 1:4, 8; 2:1–4, 33, 39; 4:8; 10:38; 11:12; Rom. 8:26).

Incarnate—The doctrine that Jesus Christ took on human form while being fully God (John 1:14; Col. 2:9).

Indwelling of Holy Spirit—The permanent residence of God within a person who professes faith in Jesus Christ as their Lord and Savior, establishing a personal and transformative relationship (John 14:15–17; Rom. 8:9; 1 Cor. 6:19; Eph. 1:13–14).

Lexicon Link—A Bible study tool focused on language and meanings of words. One looks at the original language of text and connects that specific word to other passages of Scripture. For example, see figure 16.

Lukan Theology—The study of God within Luke's writings in the gospel of Luke and Acts.

The Magnificat—Mary's song of praise found in Luke 1:46–55, which reflects joy and gratitude.

Messianic Promise—Biblical prophecies found in the Old Testament regarding a coming Messiah (Isa. 7:14; 53).

Miracle—A divine act by God where a supernatural experience overrides the natural world (figures 4 and 7).

Omnipresence—An incommunicable attribute (only possessed by God) meaning that God is present everywhere (Ps. 139:7–10; Isa. 66:1; Acts 17:27–28).

Pauline Epistles—Letters in the New Testament written by the apostle Paul to individuals and church communities sharing theology and practical matters.

Pentecost—The first Pentecost was after Jesus' resurrection and found in Acts 2:2–41, where Holy Spirit came upon all the Jewish believers and empowered them. This event is significant in biblical history as God's Promised Presence was poured out and immersed Himself as the powerful and personal Presence of God in Christ followers' lives.

Pneumatology—The study of Holy Spirit.

Prophecy—When Holy Spirit ministers divine revelation through proclaiming God's word, His will, guidance, or instruction toward past, present, or future events. This is a gift given by Holy Spirit to believers for the strengthening of the church (1 Cor. 12:10).

Prophet—A person who serves in ministry and is a messenger for God to His people sharing His truth, providing guidance, God's will, and correction through received divine revelation (1 Cor. 12:28; Eph. 4:11–16).

Providence—God's governing power, care, and involvement with creation that brings about His divine plan and purpose (Ps. 103:19; Rom. 8:28).

Sanctification—The continuous work of God that sets His followers apart as holy and conformed into His image (Rom. 6:19–22; 1 Thess. 4:3–8).

Shepherd—A person who serves in ministry and oversees and cares for the flock, the church. This role can consist of leaders in the church that serve as ministers, elders, or pastors (Eph. 4:11–16).

Signs and Wonders—Refers to supernatural events or miracles executed by God or people under God's power. Examples of signs and wonders in the Bible are healing the sick, casting out demons, raising the dead, and creative miracles.

Spiritual Gifts—Holy Spirit ministers gifts powerfully through believers for the edification and equipping of the church. The manifestations of the Spirit are words of wisdom, knowledge, prophecy, faith, gifts of healing, working of miracles, distinguishing between spirits, speaking in various kinds of tongues, and interpretation of tongues. These gifts are based on 1 Corinthians 12:7–11. Alternatively called "supernatural gifts," "gifts of the Spirit," or "charisma" (Rom. 1:11; 1 Cor. 12:1–11; 14:1).

Spiritual Warfare—The ongoing battle between good and evil in the spiritual realm. Equipped with Holy Spirit, the believer's quest is to resist the kingdom of darkness and to remain close to God as they endure in faith.

Stronghold—A place, thing, or being that has a hold over you. Often connected to spiritual warfare, strongholds are barriers and obstacles between someone and God that hold a person back from true freedom and victory. However, strongholds are not always negative. The Lord can be your stronghold too (Ps. 9:9; 18:2).

Surrender—A humbling of the soul desperate to be with God and deliberate to do what He asks (Matt. 16:24; James 4:7).

Teacher—A person who serves in ministry, instructs, and illuminates the truth of God's Word by educating with sound Christian doctrine. Teachers reveal who triune God is and how to apply biblical principles to one's life by properly interpreting Scripture (Rom 12:6–8; 1 Cor. 12:28; Eph 4:11–16).

"The Already and Not Yet"—A theological term for the tension between the present reality and the promised kingdom to come. In the already, God has won the victory over sin and death when Jesus died and rose again, but it's not yet the fullness of victory, which will one day be revealed to us at His second coming within new creation.

Topical Teaching—A type of Bible teaching that typically explores a specific theme or subject and studies related passages of Scripture in order to gain insights on the relevant topic.

Word of Knowledge—When Holy Spirit ministers divine revelation of understanding into a particular area or situation. This is a gift given by Holy Spirit to believers for the strengthening of the church (1 Cor. 12:8).

Word of Wisdom—When Holy Spirit ministers divine revelation of sound judgment, insight, or expertise of skill into a particular area or situation. This is a gift given by Holy Spirit to believers for the strengthening of the church (1 Cor. 12:8).

Working of Miracles—When Holy Spirit ministers a supernatural power that overrides the natural world. This is a gift given by Holy Spirit to believers for the strengthening of the church (1 Cor. 12:10, 28).

NOTES

Inside These Pages

1. "Luke Bible Timeline," Bible Hub, accessed July 20, 2023, https://biblehub.com/timeline/luke/1.htm; and ZA Blog, "Who Wrote the Book of Acts," *Zondervan Academic*, February 19, 2019, https://zondervanacademic.com/blog/who-wrote-the-book-of-acts.

2. "Acts Bible Timeline," Bible Hub, accessed July 20, 2023, https://biblehub.com/timeline/acts/1.htm; and ZA Blog, "Who Wrote the Book of Acts," *Zondervan Academic*, February 19, 2019, https://zondervanacademic.com/blog/who-wrote-the-book-of-acts.

3. The Holy Bible: English Standard Version (Wheaton, IL: Crossway Bibles, 2016), Acts; and Robert F. O'Toole, "Theophilus (Person)," in *The Anchor Yale Bible Dictionary*, ed. David Noel Freedman (New York: Doubleday, 1992), 511.

4. Holy Bible: English Standard Version, Luke.

5. Holy Bible: English Standard Version, Acts.

Week 1: The Wonder of God's Spirit

1. Wayne Grudem, *Systematic Theology: An Introduction to Biblical Doctrine* (Grand Rapids, MI: Zondervan Academic, 1994), 371.

2. Beth Felker Jones, *God the Spirit: Introducing Pneumatology in Wesleyan and Ecumenical Perspective* (Eugene, OR: Cascade Books, 2014), 22, Kindle edition.

3. J. I. Packer and Gary A. Parrett, *Grounded in the Gospel: Building Believers the Old-Fashioned Way* (Grand Rapids, MI: Baker Books, 2010), 14.

4. Thomas C. Oden, *Classic Christianity: Systematic Theology* (New York: HarperCollins, 2009), 4, Kindle edition.

5. Kenda Creasy Dean, *Almost Christian: What the Faith of Our Teenagers Is Telling the American Church* (New York: Oxford University Press, 2010), 63, Kindle edition.

6. Raniero Cantalamessa, *Come, Creator Spirit: Meditations on the Veni Creator* (Collegeville, MN: Liturgical Press, 2003), 190, Kindle edition.

7. Nick and Carol Marsella, video conversation with author, April 17, 2023.

Week 2: The Present Reality of God's Spirit

1. David A. deSilva, *An Introduction to the New Testament: Contexts, Methods, and Ministry Formation*, 2nd ed. (Downers Grove, IL: IVP Academic, 2018), 290.

2. A. W. Tozer, *How to Be Filled with the Holy Spirit* (Chicago: Moody, 2016), 46, Kindle edition.

3. Raniero Cantalamessa, *Come, Creator Spirit: Meditations on the Veni Creator* (Collegeville, MN: Liturgical Press, 2003), 93, Kindle edition.

4. Cantalamessa, *Come, Creator Spirit*, 159–60, Kindle edition.

5. Darrell L. Bock, *Luke*, The IVP New Testament Commentary Series (Downers Grove, IL: InterVarsity Press, 1994), Luke 4:1–13.

6. Teresa of Ávila, *The Life of St. Teresa of Jesus, of the Order of Our Lady of Carmel*, trans. David Lewis (Christian Classics Ethereal Library, 1565), chap. 12, https://ccel.org/ccel/teresa/life/life.viii.xii.html.

7. Verses where "salvation" and "saved" are mentioned in the proper context in Acts: "Salvation" 4:12; 7:25; 13:26; 13:47; 16:17; 28:28; and "saved" 2:21; 2:47; 4:12; 11:14; 15:11; 16:30–31; 27:20; 27:31.

Week 3: The Fellowship of God's Spirit

1. "The Asbury Outpouring," Asbury University, accessed July 21, 2023, www.asbury.edu/outpouring/.

2. Thomas McCall, email message to TH501 class, February 13, 2023. Also, Professor McCall released a book about the 2023 Asbury Revival: Jason E. Vickers and Thomas H. McCall, *Outpouring: A Theological Witness* (Eugene, OR: Cascade Books, 2023).

3. Saint Catherine, as quoted in Paul Murray, *Saint Catherine of Siena: Mystic of Fire, Preacher of Freedom* (Park Ridge, IL: Word on Fire Institute, 2020), 56, Kindle edition.

4. Craig S. Keener, *The IVP Bible Background Commentary: New Testament* (Downers Grove, IL: InterVarsity Press, 1993), 2 Timothy 3:5.

5. Gordon D. Fee, *Paul, the Spirit, and the People of God* (Grand Rapids, MI: Baker, 1996), 132, Kindle edition.

6. Jessie Fox, text message to author, June 28, 2023.

7. Augustine of Hippo, *Confessions*, bk. 1, ch. 1, par. 5.

8. Walter A. Elwell and Barry J. Beitzel, "Liberty," in *Baker Encyclopedia of the Bible* (Grand Rapids, MI: Baker, 1988), 1334.

Week 4: The Powerful Work of God's Spirit

1. Raniero Cantalamessa, *Come, Creator Spirit: Meditations on the Veni Creator* (Collegeville, MN: Liturgical Press, 2003), 177–78, Kindle edition.

2. Ron Clark and Dougald McLaurin III, "duty" in *Lexham Theological Wordbook*, Lexham Bible Reference Series, ed. Douglas Mangum, Derek R. Brown, Rachel Klippenstein, and Rebekah Hurst (Bellingham, WA: Lexham Press, 2014).

3. James Swanson, *Dictionary of Biblical Languages with Semantic Domains: Greek (New Testament)* (Oak Harbor, WA: Logos, 1997).

4. J. B. Green, J. Brown, and N. Perrin, *Dictionary of Jesus and the Gospels: A Compendium of Contemporary Biblical Scholarship*, 2nd ed., The IVP Bible Dictionary Series (Downers Grove, IL: IVP, 2013), 1338.

5. For biblical examples of healers, see Genesis 41:8; Exodus 7:11; Acts 13:6–12; and 19:13–16.

6. The healing accounts of Jesus after Luke 8:40–56 are in 9:11, 37–43; 11:14; 13:10–17; 14:1–4; 17:11–19; 18:35–43; and 22:50–51.

7. Minnie F. Abrams, "How Pentecost Came to India," *The Pentecostal Evangel*, no. 1619, May 19, 1945, 5.

8. Sean Gladding, *The Story of God, the Story of Us: Getting Lost and Found in the Bible* (Downers Grove, IL: InterVarsity Press, 2010), 205.

9. For example, Peter displayed the gifts: word of wisdom in Acts 10:9–48, word of knowledge in 2 Peter 3–6, prophecy in Acts 2:29–41, faith in 2 Peter 1:1, gifts of healing in Acts 3:1–10, working of miracles in Acts 5:12, distinguishing between spirits in Acts 5:1–11, speaking in various kinds of tongues in Acts 2:4, and interpretation of tongues in Acts 10:46.

NOTES

10. Priscilla was actively teaching with her husband in at least three cities. Timothy Milinovich, "Prisca," in *The Lexham Bible Dictionary*, ed. John D. Barry, David Bomar, Derek R. Brown, Rachel Klippenstein, Douglas Mangum, Carrie Sinclair Wolcott, Lazarus Wentz, Elliot Ritzema, and Wendy Widder (Bellingham, WA: Lexham Press, 2016).

11. Darrell L. Bock, *Luke*, The IVP New Testament Commentary Series (Downers Grove, IL: InterVarsity Press, 1994), Luke 9:21–27.

12. Elisabeth Elliot, *Keep a Quiet Heart* (Grand Rapids, MI: Revell, 1995), 19.

13. Timothy C. Tennent. *Invitation to World Missions: A Trinitarian Missiology for the Twenty-First Century*, Invitation to Theological Studies Series (Grand Rapids, MI: Kregel Academic & Professional, 2010), 189.

14. Sam Storms, *Understanding Spiritual Gifts: A Comprehensive Guide* (Grand Rapids, MI. Zondervan, 2020), 9–10, Kindle edition.

Bonus Material: Common Questions

1. Jenny Randle, *Getting to Know God's Voice: Discover the Holy Spirit in Your Everyday Life* (Eugene, OR: Harvest House, 2020).

A Practical Guide to Understanding the Bible

Grow in awe of God as you discover the beauty and depth of him through 31 bite-sized truths of theology. *Flash Theology* offers you stability in your faith so you can endure whatever life (or wrong thinking) throws at you.

**AVAILABLE AT DAVIDCCOOK.ORG
OR WHEREVER BOOKS ARE SOLD.**

DAVID C COOK
transforming lives together

You've just read *The Promised Presence*—now take the next step in discovering how God moves in and through you.

HOLY SPIRIT MINISTRY CENTER

The Holy Spirit Ministry Center is committed to providing the clarity, support, and resources you need to stay grounded in Scripture and guided by God's Spirit.

Gifted is our discipleship training for individuals and churches that equips believers to walk in the fullness of their spiritual gifts with biblical wisdom, godly integrity, and confidence. It's time to grow in your gifts for the glory of God and good of others.

Through the Gifted training, you will:

- **Go deeper in your faith** with this **exclusive 8-part video series and supplemental materials** taught by author and academic theologian Jenny Randle
- Understand the apostle Paul's theology around the 30 manifestations of the Spirit
- Dispel common myths surrounding spiritual gifts and understand your gift, its purpose, and its function in strengthening the church

Are you ready to embrace your gifts and walk in the Spirit with godly integrity and power?

Visit **holyspiritministrycenter.com** for info on the Gifted training, free resources, and articles on the person and work of God's Spirit.

150 YEARS STRONG
DAVID C COOK

JOIN US.
SPREAD THE GOSPEL.
CHANGE THE WORLD.

We believe in equipping the local church with Christ-centered resources that empower believers, even in the most challenging places on earth.

We trust that God is *always* at work, in the power of Jesus and the presence of the Holy Spirit, inviting people into relationship with Him.

We are committed to spreading the gospel throughout the world—across villages, cities, and nations. We trust that the Word of God will transform lives and communities by bringing light to the darkness.

As a global ministry with a 150-year legacy, David C Cook is dedicated to this mission. Each time you purchase a resource or donate, you're supporting a ministry—helping spread the gospel, disciple believers, and raise up leaders in some of the world's most underserved regions.

Your support fuels this mission.
Your partnership sends the gospel where it's needed most.

Discover more. Be the difference.
Visit DavidCCook.org/Donate